W9-AEP-448

ALL THE FRESCOS OF
RAPHAEL
Part 2
VOLUME THIRTEEN
in the
Complete Library of World Art

The Complete Library of World Art

ALL THE FRESCOS

OF **RAPHAEL**

Part 2

Edited by ETTORE CAMESASCA

Translated by PAUL COLACICCHI

LIBRARY
College of St. Francis
JOLIET, ILL.

HAWTHORN BOOKS, INC.

Publishers · New York

© 1963 by Rizzoli Editore, S.p.a. All rights reserved, including the right to reproduce this book or portions thereof in any form except for the inclusion of brief quotations in a review. All inquiries should be addressed to Hawthorn Books, Inc., 70 Fifth Avenue, New York City 11. This book is published simultaneously in Canada by McClelland & Stewart, Ltd., 25 Hollinger Road, Toronto 16. The Library of Congress has catalogued this volume of *The Complete Library of World Art* under Card Number 63–8011. Suggested decimal classification for this series: 759.

Manufactured in Great Britain by
Jarrold & Sons Ltd, Norwich

759.5
R136cc
2

CONTENTS

7-28-63

× 2 . 98

34615

These volumes deal with Raphael's *Frescos* and the reader is referred to the volumes on Raphael's *Paintings*, in the same series.

RAPHAEL'S FRESCOS

THE VATICAN STANZE (continued)

STANZA D'ELIODORO

(Plates 65–89)

This room was named after the fresco on one of its walls. Topographically speaking, it is the third, but chronologically, as regards its decoration, it was the second chamber. While the *Segnatura*'s theme was based on a spiritual concept, here the inspiration is political, though of a very high order. This chamber depicts the episodes which relate to the protection granted by God to his loyal servants from the very beginning of time. It is therefore inconceivable that Pope Julius did not personally intervene in setting out the programme of work when Raphael, perhaps in June, 1511, was entrusted with the decoration of the walls that had already been painted by Piero della Francesca, Peruzzi and Bramantino. Raphael carried out his task from the vault down to the dado upon which are painted in chiaro-

scuro eleven caryatids (representing commerce, religion, law, peace, protection, nobility, navigation, abundance, pastoral life, agriculture and vine-growing) and four herms, among which some tablets in imitation marble are visible. Under these a number of small compartments in imitation bronze refer, with numerous subjects, to the prosperity of the Church's domains. Early critics ascribed these mainly to Penni, though some believed them to have been painted by Raphael. Crowe and Cavalcaselle attribute to Penni only the caryatids, granting however, the original idea to Raphael. Modern critics attribute to Perin del Vaga the decorations along the dado. The last payment made out to Raphael for this *Stanza* was recorded on August 1, 1514.

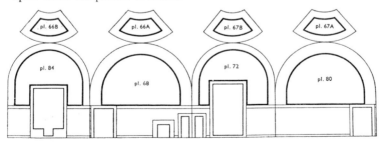

THE VAULT

(Plates 65–67)

Ribbed diagonals spring from Pope Julius II's escutcheon in the center. Along them runs a gilded strip with arabesques, framing four stories which are painted to look like canvasses fixed to their frames by means of rings and nails. The four subjects are: *The Burning Bush* (plate 66A), *Jacob's Dream* (plate 66B), *God appearing to Noah* (plate 67A), and *The Sacrifice of Abraham* (plate 67B). These themes are connected to those appearing on the walls which are: the *Expulsion of Heliodorus* (plate 68), the *Liberation of St Peter* (plate 84), the *Repulsion of Attila* (plate 80) and the *Mass of Bolsena* (plate 72). As in the story of the *Burning Bush*, an invisible God expels Heliodorus from the temple; God appears to Jacob in his dream and Peter is freed from prison during a dream; Noah seeks refuge in the Ark thanks to a divine apparition and a celestial intervention saves Rome from the fury of Attila; Abraham, who obeyed the will of God to the point of sacrificing his own son, showed a faith that was sadly lacking during the Mass of Bolsena.

The framework develops further around other episodes of a symbolic or purely decorative nature, probably painted by Peruzzi before Raphael's arrival. The four major scenes, however, were executed under Raphael's direction. Vasari and others after him, believed them to have been actually painted by the master, but Crowe and Cavalcaselle attribute their execution to Peruzzi. This opinion enjoyed some popularity until A. Venturi suggested G. de Marcillat, now generally accepted. The bad condition of the

frescos makes any clear verdict very difficult. Crowe and Cavalcaselle also observed some ornamental parts in the ceiling corners which had been repainted by Raphael's assistants. The major stories were probably executed in the second half of 1511 —in other words, before any other painting by Raphael in this chamber.

Plate 65

VAULT OF THE CHAMBER OF HELIODORUS. General view.

Plate 66A

THE BURNING BUSH. Moses is depicted kneeling as the Almighty appears to him in a whirl of flames, preceded by two cherubs and accompanied by a seraph on either side. The episode is taken from the Old Testament (Exodus III, 2–8). The influence of Michelangelo and of classical works is fairly obvious.

Plate 66B

JACOB'S DREAM. Enfolded in clouds, the Lord appears to the sleeping Patriarch at the top of a staircase lined with angels. Notice, again, signs of classical and Michelangelesque influences.

Plate 67A

GOD APPEARING TO NOAH. Floating on air, his form supported by three angels, God appears to Noah, who kneels with Ham in his arms. The Patriarch's wife is seen in the doorway of the Ark carrying Japheth and looking back towards Shem. This episode is taken from Genesis (IV, 8, 10, 13). The work was obviously influenced by the frescos in the Sistine Chapel.

THE SACRIFICE OF ABRAHAM. Isaac's father is shown standing by the altar with his right arm raised in readiness, when his wrist is gripped by an angel in flight, and a second angel darts downwards with the lamb in his arms. Left of the altar burns the sacrificial fire; to the right is the bundle of Isaac's clothes. "Classical studies hold divided sway in Raphael's mind with reminiscences of the Tuscans. . . . The kneeling Isaac bends like the stooping slave of Michelangelo in the Gallery of St Petersburg" (Crowe and Cavalcaselle).

THE EXPULSION OF HELIODORUS

(Plates 68–71)

This fresco, which was painted on a "clean" wall (Vasari), that is, a wall untouched by Raphael's predecessors, is about 15 feet wide at the base. It has given its name to the whole *Stanza*. Pope Julius II, seen on the left, instructed Raphael to develop the theme of the inviolability of the Church's temporal power, together with that of his own policy of systematically expelling all who dared usurp ecclesiastical properties. The legend of Heliodorus, as told in the Apocrypha, was particularly suited to this purpose, especially as the sacrilegious culprit of old has availed himself of an accomplice in the temple, just as the Pontiff's enemies had their own emissaries in the Curia itself. In the Temple of Jerusalem, shaped like a Greek Cross, the high priest, Onias, kneels by the altar, spilling his loot, and a celestial horseman assisted by two other heavenly messengers on foot rushes upon him. Heliodorus

has fallen to the ground on the right (plate 69). Behind them are the desecrator's men, laden with stolen goods. Amid the papal suite on the left the man nearest the frame carries a scroll inscribed: *Io. Pietro de Foliariis Cremonensis*. He was therefore assumed to be Pietro Foliari, Secretary for Papal Pleas, but the inscription was later thought to be counterfeit and the figure interpreted as a self-portrait of Raphael.

The two *Sediarii* (supporting the papal throne on their shoulders) have traditionally been identified as the engraver Raimondi, in German garb, and Giulio Romano. Vasari indeed reproduced the faces of these two figures as illustrations to their biographies. The second one, however, the so-called Giulio Romano, is probably the real self-portrait of Raphael.

It is said that during the Sack of Rome in 1527, the Spanish troops billeted in the *Stanza* used to keep a fire going just under the figure of Heliodorus, thereby causing the considerable damage which is still visible. The appalling restoration work is attributed to Maratta, but it is possible that others interfered with the fresco. Modern critics generally agree with Crowe and Cavalcaselle in considering this the first fresco to be painted on the chamber walls, about 1511–12. At one time, the fresco was thought to have been executed after the *Mass of Bolsena*. Crowe and Cavalcaselle should also be credited with having observed a great many signs of "the metallic execution of Giulio Romano" in the right section, and "the gaudy handling of Giovanni da Udine on the other." For this reason only the group consisting of the Pope and his attendants should be attributed to Raphael himself.

Gamba met with no success when he tried to restore to Raphael the authorship of all the other areas, with the exception of the background.

Perhaps the single figure of the Jew clinging to the shaft of the pillar (plate 70) could be evidence of a momentum imparted by the master to the figurative part of the scene. He may even have extended this participation to the beautiful Goya-like group of people seen beyond the youth in fluttering robes, climbing up after the Jew, and behind the Papal suite. Ortolani believes the fresco was painted in two separate periods: first the right-hand section, executed by Raphael's pupils; then, some time later, perhaps after the *Mass of Bolsena* (see appropriate comment) the left-hand section by Raphael himself.

Plate 68

EXPULSION OF HELIODORUS.

Plate 69

THE FALLEN HELIODORUS.

Plate 70

FIGURES ON THE LEFT.

Plate 71

JULIUS II. Detail of the bust.

THE MASS OF BOLSENA

(Plates 72–79 and Color Plates V and VI)

The fresco extends upward from a base of about 15 feet and comes down on both sides of the window, the span of which, at floor level, is about 4 feet.

On this wall, where Bramantino had portrayed some figures of *Condottieri*, Raphael illustrated a miracle which occurred in 1263 when a priest, traveling to Rome from Bohemia, stopped to perform Mass at the altar of Santa Cristina at Bolsena. During the Sacrifice he was overcome by doubts about the Transubstantiation, but suddenly he saw blood spurting from the Host. This miracle originated the Papal Bull of Urban IV (1264) instituting the *Corpus Domini*, and also the foundation of Orvieto's Cathedral. Tradition has it that Julius II chose this theme to honor the memory of Pope Sistus IV—who furthered the cult of *Corpus Domini*—and to celebrate the power of the Church which had emerged victoriously from the Lateran Council of May 3, 1512. If this second motive really existed, the fresco's chronology is fairly well defined, for on the soffit of the window below the *Mass of Bolsena* two false tablets bear the inscriptions: JVLIVS II. LIGVR. PONT. MAX. and ANN. CHRIST MDXII. PONTIFICAT. SVI. VIII. Among the figures and besides Pope Julius kneeling opposite the ministering priest, one recognizes (plate 75) Cardinal Riario, with crossed arms behind the Pope and, with less certainty, Cardinal Sangiorgio with his hands joined in prayer. Critics have stressed the contrast between the astonishment and agitation on the left side of the scene and the composure on the right—even the candles burn evenly here. Furthermore while the group of officials and Swiss Guards (plates 76–77) on the right is perfectly preserved, the left section shows extensive damage and restoration.

It is to the restoration, rather than to the intervention of pupils, that the painting owes a decline of quality, especially visible in the group of women. Wackernagel (*Monatshefte für Kunstwissenschaft*,

1909) claimed that Sebastiano del Piombo had executed the group of prelates (plate 75), but this was due to his misreading of a passage by Dolce (*Dialogo della Pittura*, Venice, 1557) which Pallucchini (*Sebastian Viniziano*, Milan, 1944) rightly connected to *Tribonian Handing the Code to Justinian* (see comment on plate 58, Part 1). Zampetti (*Mostra di Lorenzo Lotto*, Venice, 1953) explains the Venetian quality of the group of prelates by recalling the influence of Lotto, to whom Longhi thinks the group should be directly ascribed.

Plate 72

MASS OF BOLSENA. General view.

Plate 73

THE MINISTERING PRIEST AND SPECTATORS.

Plate 74

SPECTATORS. Detail of plate 73.

Plate 75

THE PRELATES.

Plate 76

SWISS GUARDS AND FIRST BEARER.

Plate 77

SECOND BEARER. Detail of the bust.

Plate 78

WOMEN AND CHILDREN. Detail of lower group at left.

Plate 79

JULIUS II. Detail of the head.

THE REPULSION OF ATTILA

(Plates 80–83)

Bramantino had also painted some famous *Condottieri* on this wall. Raphael's theme, composed on a base measuring about 18 feet, is the meeting between Leo I and Attila, King of the Huns, which took place in A.D. 452. They met, perhaps on the Mincio, near Mantua, but Raphael transferred the episode in his fresco to the neighbourhood of Rome. In the papal suite we see, among others, Paris de Grassis. Instead of an old man in priestly garb who, the legend has it, appeared to the invaders from the sky, Raphael has depicted the Apostles Peter and Paul (plate 81). Between the saints and the group beneath them, Rome is outlined with a Basilica, and aqueduct, the Colosseum and the *Meta Romuli*. In the center of the picture, the mounted Attila is dumbfounded at the sudden vision, which his eyes alone can see. In the background, to mark the route followed by the barbarians, a forest fire blazes on the slopes of Monte Mario. In 1513, when the fresco was already begun, Pope Julius died and Leo X succeeded him. Raphael had therefore to replace the features of Julius with those of the new Pontiff. This was not an easy task because, among other things, the head of Julius and other aspects of the picture recalled the Battle of Ravenna (April 11, 1512) which was decisive in ousting the French from Italy. As the battle had also been witnessed by Cardinal de' Medici—now Pope Leo X—the latter's face appears twice in the picture (plate 82). Crowe and Cavalcaselle believe that this fresco and the one depicting the *Liberation of St Peter* were completed after the resumption of work following Pope Julius' death—that is, in the period 1513–14—and that the *Repulsion* preceded the *Liberation*. Generally, though, the reverse order is accepted. Ortolani thinks that the *Repulsion* followed immediately after the *Expulsion of Heliodorus* and probably preceded the *Mass of Bolsena*; in his opinion, Raphael only added the papal group on the left in 1514. On the other hand, if we are to accept the allusion to the Battle of Ravenna Ortolani's chronology becomes unacceptable. The predominance of the apprentices' work, together with extensive damage, some repainting and widespread areas of darkened color make it impossible to express any opinion based on the style of the fresco. But some expert and transparent touches incline one to think that Raphael did more than paint just the head of the Pope. In addition to improvements in the horses, noticed by Gamba there are other equally successful corrections in some of the barbarians' heads and in the figures of the two Apostles descending from heaven. The credit for the lyric tonality of the Roman countryside should go to Lorenzo Lotto.

Plate 80

Color Plate V

Plate 81

Plate 82

Plate 83

THE LIBERATION OF ST PETER

(Plates 84–89)

This wall had previously been decorated by Piero della Francesca. The coincidence in concept and style between this artist's famous *nocturne*, called the *Vision of Constantine*, at Arezzo, and the episode painted by Raphael did not escape the nineteenth century critics. The fresco extends from a base measuring about 15 feet and also includes the two sides of the window, the measurements of which are the same as those of the window opposite. The picture describes two moments of the story narrated in the Acts of the Apostles: St Peter, manacled to his warders' lances, is imprisoned in Jerusalem. As he slumbers, he dreams of an angel delivering him from captivity while the guards are asleep; awakening, he realizes that he is out of prison and free. The soffit of the window below shows two imitation tablets reading: LEO X PONT. MAX. and ANN. CHRIST MDXIIII PONTIFICAT. SVI II. The year, therefore, was 1514 (see also comment on plate 80). The surface shows much repainting especially in the background. Abrasions—particularly in the lower figures, and darkening of color, increase the dense shades of night. This darkening was probably due to the work of Raphael's pupils, mainly Giulio Romano.

Plate 84

Plate 85

Plate 86

GUARDS. Detail of group at left.

Plate 87

THE ANGEL WITH THE FREE SAINT. Detail of group at right.

Plate 90

ISAIAH. *Fresco, 250 × 155. Rome, Church of Sant'Agostino, central nave, third pillar on the right.* A scroll held by the prophet bears the Greek inscription: "Open ye the gates, that the righteous nation which keepeth the truth may enter in" (Isaiah, XXVI, 2). On a tablet supported by two naked boys is the following dedication, also in Greek: "To St Anne, mother of the Virgin; to the Holy Virgin, mother of God; to Jesus the Savior, Giovanni Gorizius." This dedication was probably suggested to Raphael by the donor, the Apostolic Pronotary, John Goritz, from Luxembourg. Vasari writes that the work was almost complete when Raphael was allowed to look at Michelangelo's frescos in the Sistine Chapel. These promptly induced him "to gossip his Isaiah." This somewhat gossipy information might be connected with the partial opening of the Sistine Chapel in 1510. This would not clash with the Isaiah chronology, for the fresco is commonly dated 1511–12. The dating is not only due to reasons of style, but because the date 1512 appears beneath a statue of St Anne by Sansovino at the foot of the fresco (see the dedication above) and because the figures of the two boys were copied on behalf of Julius II (see comment on plate 91) who died on February 20, 1513. Celio informs us (*Pitture . . . in Roma*, Rome, 1638) that the fresco was accidentally washed over and later restored by

Plate 88

SLEEPING GUARD. Detail of plate 84.

Plate 89

THE ANGEL AND THE SAINT. Detail of plate 84.

Daniele da Volterra. It was undoubtedly touched up and then covered with a thick varnish which altered its appearance. Recent restoration (1959) has revealed the excellent quality of the painting. There are copies in Milan's Ambrosiana gallery (attributed to a Bolognese school), in the Vienna Kunsthistorisches Museum (wrongly ascribed to Annibale Carracci), in Dresden (by Mengs) and elsewhere.

Plate 91

CHERUB. *Detached fresco, 114 × 42. Rome, San Luca Academy.* This is a replica of the boy on the left side of *Isaiah* in the Church of Sant'Agostino, Rome. Pungileoni notes that it was painted, together with its twin (visible in *Isaiah*), on one side of the della Rovere escutcheon over a fireplace in the Vatican apartments of Pope Innocent VIII, from where it was later removed. It eventually became the property of the artist, G. B. Wicar, who, in his will of 1834, donated it to the San Luca Academy. Formerly attributed to Raphael's school (*Pungileoni*, Richardson, Passavant, Crowe and Cavalcaselle, etc.) the fresco is now usually accepted as authentic; but according to Salerno (*Bollettino d'arte*, 1960) it was probably executed by apprentices.

Plate 92

SIBYLS AND ANGELS. *Fresco, base 615. Rome, Church of Santa Maria della Pace, arch of the first chapel on the right.* From the left, and following the traditional names: the Cumaean Sibyl (plates 94 and 99) raises her hand to a prophetic scroll bearing the Greek inscription (as is the case with all the other scrolls, except the one before the last), "The Resurrection of the Dead," a winged boy (plate 94) leans upon a tablet reading: "He shall come to the light." The Persean Sibyl (plate 93) is in the act of writing, "He shall have the destiny of death." A winged boy clutches the torch of prophetic light (plates 93 and 98). An angel (plate 96) indicates to the Phrygian seer (plate 95) the motto: "The heavens surround the vase of the earth." A winged boy (plate 95 and 97) rests against a tablet inscribed in Latin: *Iam no[va] proge[nies]*. The Sibyl of Tibur has an angel flying above her with a scroll inscribed: "I shall open and I shall resurrect." Some believe that the Sibyl of Tibur should really precede the Cumaean Sibyl. This work was executed on behalf of Agostino Chigi.

Gamba assumes the date to be 1512–14, but it is generally dated 1514 for reasons of style (by Gronau, Ragghianti, Fischel, Suida and Carli among others). The fresco should therefore not be in any way connected with Chigi's will of August 28, 1519. Bocchi (*Bellezze . . . di Firenze*, Florence, 1677) wrote that Raphael demanded a fee of five hundred *scudi* and that, after expert evaluation by Michelangelo, he received twice that amount. This information is not, however, confirmed. It is generally thought wholly authentic in spite of the difficulty of analysis due to the numerous restorations and attempts to oil-polish it.

Some figures of *Prophets and Angels*

on the upper part (see drawing) are mentioned twice by Vasari in his *Life of Raphael*. Vasari attributes them and also the *Sybils* to Raphael, but in the *Life of Timoteo Viti*, he claims that the figures were invented and painted by Viti, on the evidence of those who had seen him at work, and of the cartoon owned by Viti's heirs. Consequently, some critics (Crowe and Cavalcaselle, Gamba and others) thought that one section of the wall—the one with the

Prophets—had been translated by Viti from Raphael's drawings, seen by Celio in Urbino.

A. Venturi (*Grandi artisti italiani*, Bologna, 1925) thinks, on the other hand, that both the *Prophets* and the *Sibyls* were painted by Raphael. He may have perhaps been assisted by apprentices (especially in the case of the *Sibyls*) but without the intervention of Viti. (Venturi describes Viti as "an artist of the fourteenth century, even in his last works painted in the fifteenth century.") Generally, however, the upper figures are excluded from Raphael's *corpus* and attributed to his School. The serious damage undergone by the frescos does not allow a definite verdict.

Plate 93

SIBYLS AND ANGELS. Detail of central group with the Persean Sibyl.

Plate 94

SIBYLS AND ANGELS. Detail of group at left with the Cumaean (?) and Persean Sibyls.

Plate 95

SIBYLS AND ANGELS. Detail of group at right with the Phrygian and Tibur (?) Sibyls.

Color Plate VI

THE MASS OF BOLSENA. Detail of plate 72.

Plate 96

SIBYLS AND ANGELS. Detail of angel next to the Phrygian Sibyl.

Plate 97

SIBYLS AND ANGELS. Detail of Sibyl of Tibur (?).

Plate 98

SIBYLS AND ANGELS. Detail of central boy.

Plate 99

SIBYLS AND ANGELS. Detail of Cumaean (?) Sibyl.

STANZA DELL'INCENDIO

(Plates 100–106)

This chamber is first in topographical order and third in chronological order. It was begun in the year 1514 and was understood to be completed by July, 1517. The choice of themes is a continuation and a development of the plan set out in the *Stanza d'Eliodoro* along the lines suggested by Pope Leo X (each fresco commemorates a Pope called Leo but the single "inventions" were probably suggested by Castiglione, as appears in a letter he wrote to Raphael in 1514—see Biographical Notes). Between 1507–8, Perugino painted four religious *tondi* on the ceiling, and Raphael left them untouched, either from affection for his old master (Vasari), or for reasons of "economy of time" (Crowe and Cavalcaselle), or even because there were no decorators available in his workshop (De Campos). Before deriving its name from the fresco, *Fire in the Borgo*, the chamber was called *Stanza* of the Borgia Tower.

The dado shows a series of decorations by Giulio Romano that depict,

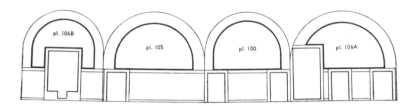

among a number of caryatids in chiaroscuro, the yellow monochrome figures of Charlemagne, Astolph, Godfrey de Bouillon, Lothair I and Ferdinand the Catholic.

FIRE IN THE BORGO

(Plates 100–104 and Color Plates VII and VIII)

The base of this fresco measures about 15 feet. The fresco illustrates a passage from the *Liber Pontificalis* about a fire which broke out in the Saxon quarter of Rome in A.D. 847 and how Pope Leo IV, by imparting his blessing from the Vatican Basilica, mastered the blaze. This episode was narrated by medieval chroniclers, but Raphael translated it into classical terms and transplanted the event to the ancient city of Troy. On the left (plate 102), followed by Creusa, Aeneas emerges from a blazing building bearing his father, Anchises, on his back and with his son, Ascanius, at his side. The Corinthian columns in this part of the fresco recall the Temple of Mars Ultor in Rome, and the erudite archaeological setting at the right brings to mind the Temple of Saturn near the Capitol. The palace from which the Pope gives his blessing (plate 104) is a fanciful and partial representation of the Vatican, while the edifice seen behind it, with mosaics on its façade, is probably a true impression of the old Basilica in Raphael's time.

Crowe and Cavalcaselle think that most of the left section was painted by Giulio Romano; the group of women in the center (plate 101) by Penni or Giovanni da Udine, and the hand of Pippi is discernible on the right. This view has been accepted by modern critics in spite of the many attempts to attribute this or that part of the painting to Raphael himself. Furthermore it has been acknowledged that Giulio Romano was also responsible for the preparatory drawing (Uffizi Gallery) of the woman bearing the vases (plate 103) at the right. Yet the head of the shouting girl exchanging vases with the man on the temple steps (plate 103), some smaller figures of imploring people in the background (plate 104) and other minute portions of the painting reveal here and there a touch worthy of Raphael himself. The fresco is usually dated 1514, which seems correct, especially if one places it in the last months of that year.

A. Venturi favors 1515. The numerous partial repaintings did not affect the columns on the left nor the background.

Plate 100

FIRE IN THE BORGO. General view.

Plate 101

WOMEN AND CHILDREN. Detail of central group in the foreground.

Plate 102

CREUSA, AENEAS, ANCHISES AND ASCANIUS. Detail of group on the left.

Plate 103

WATER BEARERS. Detail of group on the right.

Plate 104

LEO IV IMPARTING HIS BLESSING. Central scene in the background.

THE BATTLE OF OSTIA

(Plate 105)

Base approximately 770. The theme was suggested by an episode from the *Liber Pontificalis* recalling a crusade against the Turks. The Saracens, after plundering Rome in A.D. 845, threatened Ostia in A.D. 849, and Leo set out to reinforce that garrison.

The day after his return to Rome, the Saracens attacked the papal ships off Ostia, but a storm dispersed and wrecked the invaders' fleet. Raphael depicts here the Turks' annihilation after the tempest: Leo IV, with the features of Leo X, is giving thanks to God; among his courtiers are Cardinals Bibbiena and Giulio de' Medici. Behind them a road, depicting an attempted landing, leads to the citadel of Ostia; at sea, the galleys are still fighting and on the beach at the right a few Saracens are being chased. In the foreground other captives, arriving in boats, are being brought before the Pope. The fresco is commonly thought to have been executed around the end of 1514 and the beginning of the following year.

The figures in the foreground are attributed to Giulio Romano; the trophies, the architecture and the ships, to Giovanni da Udine. Raphael himself was probably responsible for the portraits of Pope Leo and the two Cardinals (Crowe and Cavalcaselle, etc.). The repainting is extensive and partly attributed to Sebastiano del Piombo by Crowe and Cavalcaselle, Gamba and others (see comment on plate 72). Some repainting is very likely by Maratta.

THE CORONATION OF CHARLEMAGNE

(Plate 106A)

Base approximately 770. It represents the ceremony which took place in A.D. 800 in the Vatican Basilica, but it probably also alludes to the 1515 Concordat of Bologna between Leo X and King Francis I of France. The investiture takes place in St Peter's depicted at the stage reached by the building when under Raphael's supervision. In the background, on the left, Pepin, Charlemagne's son, leads a group of dignitaries; next to the Emperor, who is given the likeness of Francis (just as Pope Leo III has the features of Leo X), kneels a youth whom Vasari claims to be Ippolito de' Medici; in the double row of prelates on the right Vasari identified the Bishop of Troy.

Some drawings of this fresco by Raphael exist, but the low standard of execution, aggravated as it is by restoration, abrasions and darkening of color, leads one to believe that the fresco was almost wholly the work of Penni rather than of Giovanni da Udine, as thought by earlier critics. Perhaps Penni was helped by Giulio Romano, to whom one might ascribe some figures in the left foreground. In the group of bishops at the right, in which Crowe and Cavalcaselle, and Gamba too, tended to see Raphael's hand—at least, so far as certain portraits were concerned—one now recognizes the execution of Raffaellino del Colle. In spite of the difficulties preventing a definite opinion, this painting is generally dated before the *Oath of Pope Leo III* (though other critics suggest the reverse); it was certainly carried out before the end of May, 1517 (see Biographical Notes) and after the *Battle of Ostia*.

THE OATH OF LEO III BEFORE CHARLEMAGNE

(Plate 106B)

The fresco extends from a base measuring about 15 feet and reaches down on the two sides of the window. Its subject is taken from a passage in the *Liber Pontificalis*. Leo III, on being slandered by the nephews of Adrian I, decided, "being under no compulsion and judged by no one," to justify himself publicly in St Peter's on December 23, A.D. 800. Charlemagne and the whole clergy were present when a voice cried from above: *Dei non hominum est episcopos iudicare* (these words are inscribed on the scroll at right beneath the fresco). There is, here, an obvious reference to Leo X, for the Lateran Council presided by him had confirmed, in 1516, the *Unam Sanctam* bull of Boniface VIII asserting the principle that the Pontiff should answer for his actions to God alone. In the Emperor's figure (the first on the platform to the left of the altar) Crowe and Cavalcaselle recognize the likeness of Duke Alfonso of Ferrara, and in the accuser (in profile at the opposite end of the platform) they see the features of Lorenzo de' Medici.

Nineteenth century critics attributed the large lunette section to Penni from a sketch by Raphael (Florence, Horne Foundation) and the two lower sections to Giovanni da Udine. These are now so damaged and repainted that no definite opinion can be formed. So far as the upper section is concerned, even Penni seems too distinguished for such a mediocre result. No matter how one tries, it is impossible to see in the face of the Pope and of some prelates, those "masterly touches" noted by Crowe and Cavalcaselle. Two imitation tablets on the window's soffit are inscribed: LEO. X. PONT. MAX. ANNO. CHRISTI. MCCCCCXVII, and PONTIFICAT. SVI. ANNO. IIII, from which the date 1517 was derived.

CARDINAL BIBBIENA'S BATHING ROOM

(Plate 107)

The *stufetta* or little bathroom of Cardinal Bibbiena is a small square room (252 square) with a ceiling in the shape of a cross. It is located in the apartment occupied by Bibbiena in the Vatican palace, and to which one may gain access from the third floor of the *Logge*. The east and west walls of the room are cut in the center, the one by a door and the other by a window overlooking the Pappagallo courtyard. In the center of the north and south walls are two niches framed with marble and gold which possibly contained two statuettes. Under each niche there is a marble tablet with a classical mask; from the mouth of the northern mask water pours into a basin beneath. The room's pictorial decoration, strictly classical in style, is laid out as follows: the ceilings and lunettes were painted over with light grotesques; on the sides of the door, the window and the niches, in rectangular framings of approximately 60 × 38, is a series of amorous scenes in mythological settings; these are matched below by an equal number of rectangles in which Cupids are depicted against a black background driving teams of snails (plate 107A), of dragons, turtles and butterflies. The themes of these frescos are, on the north wall, *Venus and Adonis* (plate 107B, the matching rectangle of which has been destroyed); on the east wall, the *Birth of Ericthonius* and the *Birth of Venus*; on the south wall *Venus and Cupid Riding on Dolphins* and *Venus Wounded by Cupid's Dart*; on the west wall *Pan and Syrinx*—or *Jupiter and Antiope* (the matching rectangle, possibly representing *Venus removing a thorn*, as shown in an etching by Dante, was covered with a wainscot). The date of the whole work was deduced from two letters sent by Bembo to Cardinal Bibbiena. In the first one, dated April 19, 1516, Bembo asks, on Raphael's behalf, for a second series of themes to be painted in the *stufetta*; in the second letter, date June 20 of the same year, he announces that the bathroom is now completely decorated. After Bibbiena's death, the little room was used for many different purposes and in fact remained forgotten until Pelletan described it very superficially (*Le cabinet de l'amateur*, 1844) as "the bathroom of Julius II," and

for the whole of the nineteenth century it went on being called "Pope Julius II's place of retirement."

Senneville (*Gazette des Beaux Arts*, 1874) gave it hardly more attention, so that the first real examination of the *stufetta* was due to Passavant. He was also the last critic for some years to take an interest in it. For P. Camuccini, acting on Papal orders, transformed the bathroom into a chapel, having first wainscoted the walls and covered over the ceiling with canvas. Subsequent critics therefore, were not able to form opinions until Dollmayr in 1890 and Hofmann in 1911; the former was able to identify Ovid and Servius as the sources of the themes chosen by Bibbiena and attributed the execution of the decorations to Giulio Romano, with the exception of the *Birth of Ericthonius*, which he ascribed to Penni. These attributions with the exception of the last, can be accepted as valid. As suggested by the Italian critic, De Vito Battaglia (*L'arte*, 1926), the *Birth of Ericthonius* was probably the work of an anonymous assistant of poor capability. She also thinks it possible that —because of their many points of similarity to the Galathea—the frescos of *Venus Wounded by Cupid's Dart* and *Venus and Cupid Riding on Dolphins* were derived from Raphael's sketches. Furthermore, she develops Hofmann's suggestion that the decoration in general may have been inspired by Nero's *Domus Aurea* and surmises that Giovanni da Udine may have played a part in it.

Plate 107A

CUPID DRIVING A TEAM OF SNAILS.

Plate 107B

VENUS AND ADONIS.

THE LOGGIA OF PSYCHE IN THE VILLA FARNESINA

(Plates 108–127)

Originally called the Great Lodge, this gallery (1950 × 750), on the ground floor of the Farnesina Villa in Rome had its arches open directly on to the garden so that the arbor painted on its ceiling seemed a continuation of the greenery outside (plate 108). The theme chosen by Agostino Chigi, the villa's owner, was the fable of Psyche, taken from the *Golden Ass* by Apuleius. Here (plates 109–118), the story is told of Cupid's love for the beautiful Psyche, of the jealousy of Venus and Psyche's many trials, and finally of her marriage in the presence of the placated gods. The myth is concluded in two great frescos on the ceiling (plates 126 and 127) conceived as arras hangings pinned over a frame of garlands of leaves and fruit. The garlands come down to the curved edges of the vault, to form the framework of ten spandrels (horizontal side 405) and eight lunettes (base 338) with minor subjects painted inside. The story develops from the spandrels, and the lunettes complete it with a series of Cupids (plates 119–125) celebrating the victory of Love over the various divinities whose emblems they carry. Some of the scenes are based on preparatory drawings by Raphael who, however, left the execution to his assistants. Who were they? Tatti (*Pitture di . . . Roma*, Rome, 1674) mentions also Gaudenzio Ferrari and Raffaellino del Colle. The latter's contribution (though excluded by Passavant, Crowe and Cavalcaselle) is nowadays accepted by many scholars, but Ferrari's is not, because it seems that, at the time (1515–18)

he was in Novara. The frescos are generally dated 1517, though Berenson favors 1518 and Suida 1518–19. In fact, on January 1, 1518, Sellaio, in a letter to Michelangelo, mentions the Lodge's unveiling.

The decorations have suffered so much damage that Maratta, in order to strengthen the plaster, had to secure the vault with 850 copper nails before repainting all the skies. This he did, unfortunately with patent blues, and accentuated some of the figures' outlines—revealed to this day by the many spots marring the pictures. The restorations conducted by Sartorio in 1930 were partly successful in re-establishing the pristine freshness of the skies, but several figures are still dulled by a heaviness of color for which the original artists cannot be held responsible. Fortunately, the beautiful arbor by Giovanni da Udine is practically intact.

Plate 108

THE LODGE OF PSYCHE. General view.

Plate 109

VENUS AND CUPID. Painted in the spandrel of the wall communicating with the chamber of Galatea. The Goddess bids Cupid, her son, use his dart against Psyche, who has shamed her by her greater beauty. With some doubt, Crowe and Cavalcaselle ascribe the execution to Penni; modern critics attribute it to Pippi or to Raffaellino del Colle. It seems that the work was executed by del Colle from a drawing by Pippi.

Plate 110

CUPID AND THE GRACES. First spandrel on the left of the wall towards the Chamber's interior. Cupid, who has fallen in love with Psyche, points her out to the Graces. This is generally attributed to Pippi from drawings by Raphael who—"with a light quick hand worked in Cupid's leg and the body of the nearest Grace" (Crowe and Cavalcaselle), while Giulio Romano painted the rest.

Plate 111

VENUS WITH JUNO AND CERES. Second spandrel on the inner wall. Here the theme is read in more than one way: for some critics, Venus turns in disdain from the two goddesses whose assistance against Psyche she has failed to secure; for others, she is asking the goddesses for news of her son. The execution is generally attributed to Giulio Romano.

Plate 112

VENUS IN A GOLDEN CHARIOT. Third spandrel on the inner wall. The goddess, seated in a golden chariot drawn by doves, ascends to the footstool of Jove. The execution is unanimously attributed to Pippi.

Color Plate VII

FIRE IN THE BORGO. Detail of plate 100.

Plate 113

VENUS AND JOVE. Fourth spandrel on the inner wall. Venus complains to Jove. Most critics attribute the execution to Pippi.

Plate 114

MERCURY. Spandrel on the wall communicating with the *Chamber of the Frieze.* Jove's messenger is despatched to earth with the warrant for Psyche's arrest, Venus having promised seven kisses to he who can find her hated rival. Crowe and Cavalcaselle believe lesser assistants than Pippi and Penni contributed to the execution here. They are mentioned by Vasari. A. Venturi, supported by modern critics, attributes the fresco to Pippi, though the picture's quality is definitely inferior to other parts of the cycle ascribed to him.

Plate 115

PSYCHE RETURNING FROM THE STYX. First spandrel on the left on the wall towards the garden. After her arrest, her sufferings and secret encouragements, Psyche returns from the Styx borne by Cupid's winged myrmidons and holds aloft Proserpine's love salve. Some quick sketches by Raphael remain of this. A. Venturi, supported by some recent scholars, believes the fresco to have been painted by Penni.

Plate 116

VENUS AND PSYCHE. Second spandrel on the wall looking out on the garden. Psyche presents the salve to Venus who looks at it with surprise. Sketches by Raphael are still in existence. A. Venturi assigns the execution to Penni, and some modern critics agree.

Plate 117

CUPID AND JOVE. Third spandrel on the wall looking out on the garden. Cupid pleads with the supreme judge of the gods, begging him to assuage the fury of Venus. Jupiter kisses him and promises that Psyche shall be taken by Mercury to Olympus. A drawing of this fresco, probably by Pippi, suggests the attribution of the work to that artist.

Plate 118

MERCURY AND PSYCHE. Fourth spandrel on the wall looking out on the garden. Psyche is escorted to Olympus. The execution is attributed to Penni.

Plate 119A

WINGED BOY AND EAGLE. In the lunette after the spandrel with *Venus and Cupid*. The eagle represents Jupiter and this seems confirmed by the thunderbolts. Probably executed by Raffaellino del Colle.

Plate 119B

WINGED BOY WITH TRIDENT. In the lunette before the spandrel with *Cupid and the Graces*. An allusion to Neptune. Probably executed by a minor assistant collaborating with Giulio Romano, or, it may perhaps be the work of Raffaellino.

Plate 120A

WINGED BOYS WITH CERBERUS. In the lunette between *Cupid and the Graces* and *Venus with Juno and Ceres*. The allusion to Hades is strengthened by Pluto's two-pronged fork held by the winged boy and by the presence of bats. The execution is by Pippi who left, however, the bulk of the picture to his assistants.

Plate 120B

WINGED BOY WITH ARMS. In the lunette between *Venus with Juno and Ceres* and *Venus in a Golden Chariot*. The allusion to Mars is made obvious by the sword and shield and also by the hawks in the foreground.

This fresco, possibly executed by Giulio Romano's apprentices, is in very poor condition.

Plate 121A

WINGED BOY AND GRIFFIN. In the lunette between *Venus in a Golden Chariot* and *Venus and Jove*. The bow and quiver refer to Apollo (Passavant). The execution is by Giulio Romano's assistants.

Plate 121B

WINGED BOY WITH CADUCEUS. In the lunette after the spandrel with *Venus and Jove*. The allusion to Mercury is also underlined by the winged helmet in the boy's left hand. Probably the work of Penni or carried out under his guidance.

Plate 122A

WINGED BOY AND PANTHER. In the lunette before the spandrel with *Mercury*. The allusion to Bacchus is stressed by the thyrsus borne by the boy. There are, in this fresco, elements of style recalling the previous lunette, but its bad condition hampers an opinion.

Plate 122B

WINGED BOY WITH PIPE OF REEDS. In the lunette following the spandrel with *Mercury*. It depicts Pan on the left, some birds fly round an owl.

Plate 123A

WINGED BOY WITH SHIELD AND HELMET. In the lunette before the spandrel with *Psyche Returning from the Styx*. In the opinion of Bellori the arms are those of Alexander the

Great, but Förster (*Farnesinastudien*, Leipzig, 1892) thinks they belong to Perseus. Passavant believes the helmet to represent Minerva and the shield an Amazon. The execution is probably by Penni or his apprentices.

Plate 123B

WINGED BOY WITH SHIELD AND HELMET. In the lunette between *Psyche Returning from the Styx* and *Venus and Psyche*. Förster (see above) interprets the martial symbols as an allusion to Perseus; Passavant, to Mars himself. Probably executed by Giulio Romano's apprentices.

Plate 124A

WINGED BOYS AND HARPY. In the lunette between *Venus and Psyche* and *Cupid and Jove*. The club held aloft by the boys alludes to Hercules; Förster believes the Harpy to be Echidna. The execution was carried out under the guidance of Giulio Romano.

Plate 124B

WINGED BOY WITH CROCODILE. In the lunette between *Cupid and Jove* and *Mercury and Psyche*. The hammer and pincers allude to Vulcan. This fresco, in poor condition, was probably carried out under the guidance of Penni.

Plate 125A

WINGED BOY, LION AND SEA-HORSE. In the lunette following the spandrel with *Mercury and Psyche*. In the opinion of Passavant it represents the triumph of love over all the inhabitants of the earth and the sea. Executed by Pippi or by his apprentices.

Plate 125B

WINGED BOY WITH BOW. In the lunette before the spandrel with *Venus and Cupid*. The central boy grips the bow and points to the arrows in his quiver. The fresco symbolizes Love. Executed by Giulio Romano, perhaps from a drawing by Raphael.

Plate 126

THE COUNCIL OF THE GODS. On the ceiling. Jupiter sits in judgment with Diana, Juno and Pallas on one side and Neptune, Vulcan and Mars at the other; in front of him Venus accuses Psyche, and Cupid pleads for her; next to Mars are Apollo, Hercules, Janus and other minor gods; on the left Psyche's knees are hugged by a winged boy; Mercury hands her the cup of immortality. Some preparatory drawings by Giulio Romano favor the theory that he painted at least the right side of the fresco. Some figures on the left might have been executed by Penni. Gamba would ascribe the whole of this and the following work to Penni. Judgment is hampered by the fresco's poor condition.

Plate 127

THE WEDDING BANQUET. On the ceiling. Venus dances to the music of Apollo watched by the Muses; the gods sit at the table. Jupiter is handed a cup of nectar by Ganymede, while the Hours drop flowers upon the merry party. Psyche sits between Jupiter and Cupid, and the Graces pour scent over her head. Bacchus is busily filling more cups proffered by winged boys. This fresco, for which there are several preparatory sketches by Raphael, is also in very bad condition and cannot be clearly analyzed. Penni's hand, however, can be detected in some of the figures.

THE LOGGE

(Plates 128–153)

Raphael's *Logge* form the second storey of a building originally consisting of two rows of superimposed arches, designed by Bramante for Julius II as the east façade of Nicholas III's palace in the Vatican. The construction was probably begun in 1512 (De Campos), and continued during the reign of Leo X. At Bramante's death in 1514, Raphael succeeded him and, by 1519, had not only remodeled the second, but built a third *Loggia*. The change of architect probably took place when the middle storey had just been begun, and Raphael was thus able—without ignoring his predecessor's ideas—to proceed "with greater method and ornament" (Vasari), presumably stressing the building's classical inspiration. The *Logge* consist of thirteen arches (total length approximately 650, width 400). Each arch has a small vault with four frescos (base of each fresco 140). The first twelve groups of frescos depict stories from the Old Testament (plates 128–151) and the last one shows four scenes from the New Testament (plates 152–153); thus we have a total of fifty-two frescos forming the so-called "Bible of Raphael." In the middle of the central vault we see the escutcheon of Leo X; in the others there are victories or other symbols exalting Cardinal de' Medici before he became Pope.

The episodes in the first and thirteenth vaults are enclosed in hexagonal frames, with small figures of angels in various attitudes in the lower corners. The scenes in the remaining vaults are surrounded by rich frames, arched or rectangular, in colored or gilded stucco, with grotesques or architectural decorations in the corners, of a taste very similar to that of Peruzzi's Villa Farnesina columns. Grotesques and other ornaments run all along the walls and pilasters in what Crowe and Cavalcaselle describe as "undoubtedly the most remarkable decorative work of the fourteenth and fifteenth centuries." On the first arch of the north side we see what has been described as Raphael's workshop. The same theme with variations inspires other compositions. On the third pillar, towards the courtyard, a medallion purports to show Michelangelo. On the fourth arch Leo X is seen blessing a prelate in the Loggia itself; other stuccos reproduce famous works such as Donatello's *St George*, the *Apollo of Belvedere* and *Jonah* in the Church of Santa Maria del Popolo designed by Raphael and executed by Lorenzetto. The elephant Hanno (see Lost Frescos) is reproduced twice, but most subjects are of a mythological nature. The ornaments on the skirting frame are a series of monochromes also of biblical inspiration.

In spite of diversity of opinion, most critics agree that the paintings in the vaults were executed under the direction of Giulio Romano and Penni, who in their turn were supervised by Raphael. To these names those of Giovanni da Udine and Perin del Vaga were added, mainly because of their reputation in the ornamental field, together with other minor artists recorded by Vasari: Pellegrino da Modena, Vincenzo da San Gemignano, Tommaso Vincidor called *il Bologna*, Polidoro da Caravaggio, who was then still a boy, and perhaps, Raffaellino del Colle. The most elaborate grotesques are attributed to Perin del Vaga. The others are by Giovanni da Udine, who also executed the stuccos—it was he who had rediscovered the classical way of preparing that substance with quick-lime and marble powder. The idea for the *Logge*'s ornaments was partly inspired by Nero's *Domus Aurea*, which had come to light only a short time before.

The date, 1513, inscribed under a stucco of a *Victory*, on the left side of a window in the twelfth arch, is not to be connected with the pictorial work. Dollmayr (*Archivio storico dell' arte*, 1890) stated that the cycle was begun in the last months of 1517, and many later writers share that opinion, though Fischel and Carli prefer 1518 (see Biographical Notes), and Gamba, 1516. One can, however, safely assume that the work was finished during the first half of 1519, for on June 11 of that year, 25 ducats were paid "to the youths who have painted the Loggia" (Vatican Archives). Five days later, Castiglione wrote Isabella Gonzaga that "a painted *Loggia* is now completed in the Vatican, and is the work of Raphael." On May 4, Michiel had passed the same information on to a correspondent in Venice.

Time and weather (for the *Loggia* was enclosed with glass only in the second half of the nineteenth century) have inflicted many injuries on the decorations, the lower part of which has mostly disappeared. The frescos in the vaults have been badly restored more than once. The stuccos were subjected, from 1800, to various treatments aimed to preserve them. In 1952, two painted half-pillars were discovered behind the wall erected during the reign of Paul III (1534-49) which seals off the last arch of the *Loggia*. We can now enjoy those masterpieces in all their original splendor.

Plate 128A

GOD SEPARATING LIGHT AND DARKNESS. *First small vault*. In spite of the difficult analysis due to damage, Crowe and Cavalcaselle believe it the work of Giulio Romano and Penni. Nowadays the tendency is to attribute it to Penni, perhaps from a drawing by Pippi.

Plate 128B

GOD SEPARATING LAND AND WATERS. *First small vault*. Crowe and Cavalcaselle describe it as "a fine conception worked out with Raphaelic feeling by Giulio Romano." Modern critics view it in the same light as the previous fresco. Gamba thinks that it was probably painted by Raphael as a start to the whole cycle. The fresco shows considerable damage.

Color Plate VIII

FIRE IN THE BORGO. Detail of plate 100.

Plate 129A

GOD CREATING THE SUN AND MOON. *First small vault*. Though considering it "more feeble than the previous ones," Crowe and Cavalcaselle would ascribe the fresco to Giulio Romano. Modern critics, again see in it the hand of Penni, presumably from a drawing by Pippi.

Plate 129B

GOD CREATING ANIMALS. *First small vault*. Crowe and Cavalcaselle see the work of Giulio Romano in

73

the figure of God and believe that the animals may have been drawn from studies by Giovanni da Udine. Modern critics tend to apply the same attributions here as in the case of the previous frescos.

The four paintings in this vault are framed, at the corners, with lozenges containing half-lengths of angels believed by Fischel to be the only evidence of Raphael's work in the *Logge*. The monochrome in the skirting, which Vasari attributes to Perin del Vaga, together with all the other monochromes, depicts *God Blessing the Seventh Day*.

Plate 130A

CREATION OF EVE. *Second small vault*. The landscape has been sadly marred by abrasions; the rabbit at Adam's feet is said to symbolize fecundity. Vasari, supported by Crowe and Cavalcaselle, attributes this fresco to Giulio Romano. Modern critics favor Penni, perhaps assisted by Giulio. The beautiful nude of Eve has been found to be strongly suggestive of Raphael's manner.

Plate 130B

ORIGINAL SIN. *Second small vault*. Crowe and Cavalcaselle attribute to Giulio Romano not only the execution but also the fresco's conception, though they assume that he may have been assisted by Penni. Guzzi (in *Civiltà*, July 21, 1941) ascribes it with some doubt to Pippi. A. Venturi favors Penni and so do modern critics some of whom, however, accept the hypothesis of Pippi's assistance.

Plate 131A

EXPULSION OF ADAM AND EVE. *Second small vault*. Crowe and Cavalcaselle see in the figure of Eve "the coarser shaping of Giulio." Modern critics favor an attribution to Penni, assisted perhaps by Giulio Romano.

Plate 131B

ADAM AND EVE AT WORK. *Second small vault*. Eve spins, seated under a tree, with her two children and a dog nearby. Adam sows his field. Any analysis is made difficult by the extensive damage sustained by the fresco. The monochrome below, which has perished, represented: *Cain and Abel Kneeling at their Altars*, *God the Father Confronting Abel* and, to the right, *Cain Slaying his Brother*.

Plate 132A

THE BUILDING OF THE ARK. *Third small vault*. Crowe and Cavalcaselle attribute the composition of the fresco to Giulio Romano, but the greater part of its execution to Penni. Vasari had previously ascribed the whole work to Romano. Modern critics agree with Crowe and Cavalcaselle, though some believe that Giovanni da Udine had a part in the painting of the landscape.

Plate 132B

DELUGE. *Third small vault*. A man, riding a swimming horse, approaches a nude male with a lifeless woman in his arms, while another bearded man with a child in his grasp steps out of the water dragging after him by the hair a second woman also carrying a child. In the background the ark looms large in the stormy atmosphere. Crowe and Cavalcaselle assign this to Giulio Romano, including the composition, though they make the point that Raphael supervised the execution and that the whole work was inspired by Paolo Uccello's paintings and by classical statues.

Modern critics prefer Penni, assisted perhaps by Giulio and by Giovanni da Udine so far as the landscape is concerned.

Plate 133A

NOAH LEAVES THE ARK. *Third small vault.* The animals, proceeding in couples, walk away from the vessel, or fly up in the sky, watched by Noah and his family. The injuries to the upper part of the painting make any analysis impossible. Crowe and Cavalcaselle assume that the animals were painted by Giovanni da Udine.

Plate 133B

NOAH'S SACRIFICE. *Third small vault.* Vasari attributes this work to Giulio Romano who, in the opinion of Crowe and Cavalcaselle, may have sketched the composition "with suggestions by Raphael." The execution is by Penni, though the animals, as before, may have been painted by Giovanni da Udine. This theory is generally accepted by modern critics. The monochrome in the skirting, designed presumably by Pippi, shows *Noah Gazing at the Rainbow.*

Plate 134A

ABRAHAM AND MELCHIZEDECH. *Fourth small vault.* King Melchizedech and his attendants bring baskets of bread and jugs of wine to Abraham, who appears in Roman helmet and arms, at the head of his own people. The landscape has been said to recall the Tiber valley near Rome. Crowe and Cavalcaselle attribute this fresco to Giulio assisted by Penni. Modern critics accept their theory, pointing out that the execution is mainly by Penni.

Plate 134B

GOD'S PROMISE TO ABRAHAM. *Fourth small vault.* In the view of Crowe and Cavalcaselle the composition of this fresco is by Giulio, the execution by Penni. This attribution is mainly accepted by modern critics. Many injuries have been sustained by this fresco.

Plate 135A

ABRAHAM AND ANGELS. *Fourth small vault.* The landscape recalls the valley of the Tiber near Rome. The attributions are the same as in the case of the previous fresco.

Plate 135B

FLIGHT OF LOT. *Fourth small vault.* Lot, giving his hands to his daughters, is seen escaping from the burning city of Sodom while, behind them, his wife turns to look at the flames and is turned into a pillar of salt. A. Venturi ascribes this fresco to Penni and so do modern critics some of whom, however, detect traces of Pippi's work. The monochrome beneath the frescos represents the *Sacrifice of Abraham,* and its composition, in the opinion of Crowe and Cavalcaselle, is probably derived from Raphael himself.

Plate 136A

GOD APPEARS TO ISAAC. *Fifth small vault.* On the left, with her face resting on her hand, is Rebecca. Crowe and Cavalcaselle attribute this work to Giulio Romano. Modern critics agree, though insisting that Penni contributed to the figures, and Giovanni da Udine to the landscape. Many copies on wood, executed by Giulio himself, are in existence.

Plate 136B

ISAAC AND REBECCA ARE SPIED UPON BY ABIMELECH. *Fifth small vault.* The current tendency is to assign the composition to Giulio Romano and the execution to Penni, though some recent critics, struck by the fresco's beauty, stress the analogy with Raphael's own style.

Plate 137A

ISAAC BLESSING JACOB. *Fifth small vault.* Guided by Rebecca, Jacob places a dish to the right of his father's couch, while Isaac blesses him. Esau enters on the far left, carrying a slain kid. The scheme seems to have been devised by Pippi and executed by Penni.

Plate 137B

ISAAC AND ESAU. *Fifth small vault.* Having laid the kid on the floor, Esau now asks for Isaac's blessing. The Patriarch is still lying upon his couch and, by the door, Rebecca explains the incident to Jacob. The same attributions hold good here as for the previous fresco. This one, however, is badly damaged. The monochrome on the skirting below repeats the theme of *Esau before Isaac.* Passavant believes that a sketch by Raphael was mistakenly copied twice.

Plate 138A

JACOB'S DREAM. *Sixth small vault.* Traditionally assigned to Pellegrino da Modena, but now thought to have been painted by Penni from a drawing by Giulio Romano who—in the opinion of Crowe and Cavalcaselle —may well have drawn his inspiration from Raphael's sketches for the ceiling of the *Stanza d'Eliodoro* and probably took part in the very fine execution.

Plate 138B

JACOB MEETS RACHEL. *Sixth small vault.* Rachel and a female companion stand by the fountain where Jacob's flock are drinking water. Traditionally assigned to Bernardino da Modena, but Crowe and Cavalcaselle apply to it the same remarks put forward in respect of the *Dream.* A. Venturi attributes it to Penni, whose manner however appears more stressed here than in *Jacob's Dream.* The landscape has been ascribed to Giovanni da Udine. De Campos remarks on the fresco's high quality and the outstanding quality of execution throughout the cycle.

Plate 139A

JACOB BEGS FOR THE HAND OF RACHEL. *Sixth small vault.* Laban, Rachel's father, indicates to Jacob by raising seven fingers that, if he wishes to marry Rachel, he shall first have to spend seven years in his service. Jacob repeats the gesture to his beloved, who is standing shyly behind him. In spite of the fresco's bad condition Crowe and Cavalcaselle recognize in it the work of Penni under the guidance of Pippi, and possibly with the help of others. This is accepted by modern critics who also believe that Giovanni da Udine contributed to the landscape.

Plate 139B

JACOB ON THE WAY TO CANAAN. *Sixth small vault.* Ascribed by A. Venturi to Pippi. This opinion is generally accepted. The monochrome below shows *Jacob Wrestling with the Angel* between the sleeping Rachel and two shepherds resting on the ground.

Plate 140A

JOSEPH INTERPRETS THE DREAMS TO HIS BROTHERS. *Seventh small vault*. The two dreams are outlined in the two disks on each side of the palm tree: an old man in a field between the sun and moon, and a field with sheaves. A. Venturi attributes this to Pippi but more recent critics support the theory of Crowe and Cavalcaselle who think the composition to be by Giulio and the execution by Giulio and Penni, with Giovanni da Udine responsible for the landscape.

Plate 140B

JOSEPH IS SOLD BY HIS BRETH-REN. *Seventh small vault*. The same attributions hold good as for the previous fresco.

Plate 141A

JOSEPH IS TEMPTED BY POTI-PHAR'S WIFE. *Seventh small vault*. In spite of its injuries this fresco reveals many of the features observed in the two previous works.

Plate 141B

JOSEPH BEFORE PHARAOH. *Seventh small vault*. The dreams of the fat and lean kine, and the fat and lean years are represented in two disks above the architecture of the room. They symbolize seven years of prosperity and seven years of famine. The critics share the same opinions about this fresco as expressed in the case of the three previous ones. The monochrome below shows *Joseph Revealing himself to his Brothers*.

Plate 142A

FINDING OF MOSES. *Eighth small vault*. Vasari, supported by A. Venturi, attributes this fresco to Giulio Romano, who may indeed have conceived it. It was executed with the help of Penni.

Plate 142B

THE BURNING BUSH. *Eighth small vault*. The same attributions hold good as in the previous fresco.

Plate 143A

CROSSING OF THE RED SEA. *Eighth small vault*. A. Venturi, supported by some modern critics, sees here the work of Pippi. Crowe and Cavalcaselle prefer Perin del Vaga in respect of both the composition and the execution. This theory has correctly been accepted by several recent scholars.

Plate 143B

MOSES STRIKING THE ROCK. *Eighth small vault*. Crowe and Cavalcaselle put forward Giulio Romano assisted perhaps by Polidoro da Caravaggio, but most modern experts prefer Penni to Polidoro. The monochrome below shows the *Gathering of Manna*.

Plate 144A

MOSES RECEIVING THE TABLES OF THE LAW. *Ninth small vault*. Taja (*Descrizione del . . . Vaticano*, Rome, 1750) attributes this fresco and the three following ones to Raffaellino del Colle who, however, was not mentioned by Vasari to be among Raphael's assistants in the *Logge*. Other critics thought they could detect, in the whole of this ninth vault, the work of Gaudenzio Ferrari, on the strength of information provided by Titi (*Descrizione delle pitture . . . in Roma*, Rome, 1674 and 1763). Crowe and Cavalcaselle prefer Pippi, perhaps assisted by

Penni, and most modern critics, including L. Venturi (*L'arte*, 1926), share this view.

Plate 144B

THE WORSHIP OF THE GOLDEN CALF. *Ninth small vault.* The same attribution is valid as in the previous fresco.

Plate 145A

THE COLUMN OF SMOKE. Kneeling outside his tent, Moses addresses the Eternal Father, concealed in a column of smoke. This fresco is sadly damaged and in the view of Crowe and Cavalcaselle—who do not, however, hazard an attribution —"seems executed by a mediocre hand." Modern critics favor Pippi assisted by Penni.

Plate 145B

MOSES DISPLAYS THE TABLES. *Ninth small vault.* Concerning the attribution, see comment on plate 144A. The monochrome in the skirting, in Passavant's opinion, represented *Joshua Addressing the People of Israel.*

Plate 146A

CROSSING OF THE JORDAN. *Tenth small vault.* The winding Israelite army, led by a captain in Roman armor, marches towards the Jordan. Their standard bears the arms of Leo X. The river is guarded by a seated divinity. Vasari attributes this fresco to Perin del Vaga and modern critics agree. The same artist's hand is visible in the other frescos of this vault and in the three which follow.

Plate 146B

FALL OF JERICHO. *Tenth small vault.* Platner observes that the

biblical text has not been strictly followed, for the charge is sounded by drummers and not by trumpeters. Crowe and Cavalcaselle believe that Perin del Vaga may have been helped by others in this particular work. The fresco is in good condition.

Plate 147A

JOSHUA ARRESTS THE COURSE OF THE SUN AND MOON. *Tenth small vault.* Crowe and Cavalcaselle, though accepting Vasari's attribution to Perin del Vaga as far as the execution is concerned—modern critics would agree with this— associate the scheme with a cartoon by Giulio Romano.

Plate 147B

ALLOTMENT OF THE PROMISED LAND. *Tenth small vault.* Seated under a dais, and attended by the high priest Eleazar, Joshua supervises the allotment of new lands to the Israelites. A youth draws the lots from two urns. With regard to attributions see comment on plate 146A. The fresco is partly damaged. Bartoli, who copied the *Logge* monochromes, stated that the tenth monochrome was the one representing two standing figures and two runners at the sides of a door. Crowe and Cavalcaselle, however, observe that there could not be a monochrome under this vault, for in that particular spot there is a door leading to the Hall of the *Palafrenieri*.

Plate 148A

ANOINTING OF DAVID. *Eleventh small vault.* Near an altar upon which the sacrificial fire and the ram are being prepared, Samuel anoints David in the presence of his four brothers. Supported by modern critics, Crowe and Cavalcaselle attribute the execution to Perin del Vaga, possibly from a drawing by Penni.

Plate 148B

DAVID AND GOLIATH. *Eleventh small vault.* The attributions are the same as those for the previous plate, but Crowe and Cavalcaselle believe that the preparatory drawing for this fresco was done by Pippi, perhaps based on an idea which Raphael derived from the Sistine Chapel.

Plate 149A

TRIUMPH OF DAVID. *Eleventh small vault.* This is considered one of the best frescos by Perin del Vaga in the *Logge* cycle. Crowe and Cavalcaselle think that Giulio Romano was responsible for the composition which he derived from a bas-relief on the Arch of Titus at Rome.

Plate 149B

DAVID SEES BATHSHEBA. *Eleventh small vault.* Bathsheba is combing her hair; David sees her from his window under which the Israelite army is marching to engage the Ammonites. The attributions are the same as for plate 148A. The monochrome in the skirting, which Bartoli describes as the *Propagation of the Gospel*, probably represented an episode from the life of Joshua.

Plate 150A

ANOINTING OF SOLOMON. *Twelfth small vault.* The bearded river-god symbolizes the Jordan, though the tiger at his side is generally associated with the river Tigris (Passavant). Modern critics attribute the execution to Perin del Vaga, but a more reliable opinion appears to be that of Crowe and Cavalcaselle. These recognize in the fresco the

character of *Moses Striking the Rock* in the eighth small vault, though remarking that here "the modeling is defective and the outlines look empty." Pippi, in their opinion, executed this scene with the help, perhaps, of Polidoro da Caravaggio. The composition is undoubtedly Pippi's. Some earlier historians saw in this work the work of Pellegrino da Modena; they based this theory on vague items of information provided by Vasari, although Vasari's comments were not connected with this particular vault.

Plate 150B

SOLOMON IN JUDGMENT. *Twelfth small vault.* Rather than by Perin del Vaga, to whom it is generally assigned, this appears to have been executed by the same hand responsible for the previous fresco.

Plate 151A

SOLOMON RECEIVES THE QUEEN OF SHEBA. *Twelfth small vault.* The execution is generally attributed to Perin del Vaga. Crowe and Cavalcaselle believe him also responsible for the preparatory drawing.

Plate 151B

BUILDING OF THE TEMPLE. *Twelfth small vault.* Solomon and his courtiers study the plan of the temple of Jerusalem while the men are busily working. The buildings on the left recall the architecture of the Pantheon and the column of Trajan or Antoninus. This fresco is sadly damaged and little or nothing remains of the figures of Solomon, his courtiers, and the man on the right who is goading two buffalos pulling a boulder. Generally attributed to Perin del Vaga. Crowe and Cavalcaselle believe that the style recalls that of the first two frescos in this vault (plates 150B and 151A). The charming *silhouettes* seen through the arch at the right are possibly the work of Giovanni da Udine or one of his assistants. The monochrome in the skirting represents *David and Bathsheba*.

Plate 152A

ADORATION OF THE SHEPHERDS. *Thirteenth small vault*. Vasari, who omitted, however, to mention the following fresco of the *Epiphany*, attributes this vault to Perin del Vaga and this was accepted by critics throughout the centuries, including A. Venturi. Filippini (*Bollettino d'arte*, January, 1929), suggested Bologna, but this theory was later received with great reservation. The

fresco has been visibly damaged by time.

Plate 152B

EPIPHANY. *Thirteenth small vault*. Very similar in style to the previous fresco and subject, therefore, to the same comments. It is very well preserved.

Plate 153A

BAPTISM OF CHRIST. *Thirteenth small vault*. See comment on previous plate.

Plate 153B

LAST SUPPER. *Thirteenth small vault*. The attribution is the same as for the previous three frescos, though Filippini sees in it the work of Tommaso Vincidor. The monochrome below represents the *Resurrection of Christ*.

THE VATICAN LOGGETTA

(Plates 154–156)

This cycle is situated in a long rectangular chamber (1574 × 312; height 4604 from the floor to the summit of the rounded vault), at the level of the third Vatican *Loggia* and actually built against it at the point where it juts out towards the square of St Peter's (see plan on page 33). One enters it from the south, through one of the shorter walls. The architectural plan of this story, and especially of the *Loggetta* was drawn by Raphael, as proved by De Campos (1946) who was also successful in establishing its approximate date. On one of its two larger walls three arches look down on the Maresciallo courtyard; between the arches are four arched windows (see plate 154). The opposite wall shows a symmetrical effect: the great arches

are matched by similar partitions, whilst three false niches face the windows (one of them, the first one from the entrance, was replaced by a door); in each niche a female figure, having the illusion of a classical statue, is painted against a purple background. The first figure must have represented *Winter*, for the other three symbolize *Autumn* (plate 155B), *Summer* and *Spring*. These niches are bracketed by eight slender columns, four on each side, painted on the wall and giving the impression of supporting a similarly painted structure divided into compartments. Slightly above the center columns a painted shelf supports a number of small figures, grouped and isolated: two winged divinities next to the second niche from the door, two women spinning near the third niche (see comment on plate 155A), two scenes depicting pagan rites by the fourth one (see comment on plate 155A).

The compartments opposite the great arches are entirely decorated with grotesques painted around three short rectangles (plate 155C). The grotesques, the greater part of which have perished, spread to the other surfaces, such as the ceiling, the intervals between the windows and arches, the curves of the columns and of the arched windows. In the middle of this intricate network of architectural and vegetable elements, the eye travels—as in the *Logge*—to the reproductions of famous statues (the Brescia *Victory* and Sansovino's *Bacchus* upon the ceiling), or of the animals Leo X loved (a giraffe, the ever-present elephant, Hanno, etc.). The ceiling is also lined at its highest point with horizontal festoons, and decorated with three small circular sections, extremely damaged, at the top of every arch. Above the windows and the false niches, more columns support some slender *aedicules* containing statuettes. On the skirting along the four walls runs a series of compartments decorated with scenes or geometrical representations: in spite of the damage one can still see, in the third compartment, *Venus with Cupid* (?), in the thirteenth *Mucius Scaevola*, in the sixteenth a *Weeping Woman*, in the seventeenth a *Bullfight*, in the eighteenth a *Greyhound*.

The decoration was devised by Raphael and executed, under his supervision, by Giulio Romano, Penni, Perin del Vaga and Giovanni da Udine, probably assisted by minor artists. Steinmann (*Kunstchronic*, 1905–6, and *Museumskunde*, 1906) noted the extent of Raphael's

influence on Giovanni da Udine who is correctly described as the painter of the grotesques (though in this he was partly helped by others). The allegories of the *Seasons* were designed by Penni and painted by an assistant (De Campos). The lunette above the entrance, badly damaged and representing a group of *Dancing Women*, appears to have been devised and perhaps even painted by Giulio Romano, as confirmed by the similarity of style to other drawings by Romano (Dollmayr, *Jahrbuch der kunthistorisches Sammlungen des allerh. Kaiserhauses*, 1895). The lunette on the opposite wall, with *Vulcan's Forge* (plate 156), reveals similarities of style to the *Seasons*, and should therefore be attributed to Penni, at least in so far as the composition is concerned. Of the figures inside the *aedicules* near and above the windows, the *Winged Divinities* next to *Autumn* seem to be by Pippi; the *Woman with Distaff* (plate 155A) and the *Woman with Bobbin*, next to *Summer*, and the two scenes depicting *Pagan Rites* next to *Spring* were presumably devised and painted by Perin del Vaga.

The compartments inside the arched sections—opposite the real arches—on the inner wall, represented in lively colors against a black background: *Olympus Pleads with Apollo* (plate 155C) and the *Contest between Apollo and Marsyas*. These were designed and painted by Pippi. A third compartment, now lost, probably represented the *Flaying of Marsyas*. This was established by De Campos on the strength of the sixteenth century *Codex Pighianus*, now in Berlin, and illustrating compositions of a *Colombarium* from which these scenes were derived. This has now been destroyed.

The date of execution of all these works is made available in a letter written by Michiel from Rome on May 4, 1519. It reads: "Raphael of Urbino has decorated in the [Vatican] Palace four of the Pope's chambers [*Stanze*] and a very long *Loggia* [the second one, known as the *Logge*]. He is now decorating two more *Logge*." The *Loggetta* must have been one of these two because, if one of them was the *Loggia* on the ground floor, the other one could not have been the gallery on the third floor. The decorations for the latter, though possibly designed by Raphael, were certainly executed by Giovanni da Udine after 1550 (De Campos). Michiel's letter might lead one to suppose that Raphael took an active part in the *Loggetta*'s decorations but, as De Campos claims, while in the *Logge* "some partial intervention by Raphael, at least with sketches or drawings, may be assumed, nothing warrants such a supposition in this case [of the *Loggetta*]."

This shorter gallery or, as they called it at the time, the "Corridor," was used for a long time as living quarters, and divided into rooms by two partitions, demolished in December, 1906. The decorations were found under the layers of plaster, and the discovery was announced by Steinmann. He, however, submitted the idea that what had come to light was a lost *Aviary* commissioned by Julius II from Baldassarre Peruzzi. The date, 1519, in Michiel's letter and other argu-

ments by De Campos have proved Steinmann wrong. The interest in this discovery soon faded and no restorations were continued—except for a bad repainting of the ceiling—until 1943–6, during which period the whole *Loggetta* was accurately and intelligently restored. The ornamental parts which could safely be reconstructed were repainted in lighter tones, so that the repairs could remain visible. One of the rectangular framings and its inner space in one of the larger arched sections was entirely redone, and all the areas from which the plaster had gone were painted over anew.

Plate 154
THE VATICAN LOGGETTA. View of wall overlooking the Maresciallo courtyard.

Plate 155
WOMAN WITH DISTAFF. In the false *aedicula* on the left of *Summer*.

Plate 155B
AUTUMN. In the second false niche on the innermost long wall.

Plate 155C
OLYMPUS PLEADS WITH APOLLO. Center compartment in the first arched section of the wall mentioned above.

Plate 156
VULCAN'S FORGE. Lunette on the wall opposite the entrance.

SALA DI COSTANTINO

(Plates 157–159)

This hall, once called the "Superior Hall of the Pontiffs," is topographically part of Raphael's *Stanze* (see plan on page 33) but its decoration, though conceived by Raphael, was carried out by his apprentices mainly after his death. The work was commissioned by Pope Leo X in 1517, and was finished by early September, 1524. The frescos illustrate the end of Paganism and the official establishment of the Church in Rome. This concludes the historical and political program suggested by Leo himself. The four main frescos represent: the *Baptism of Constantine* (plate 159B), the *Vision of the Cross* (plate 158C), the *Victory over Maxentius* (plate 157) and the *Gift of Rome to the Papacy* (plate 159A). They simulate vast tapestries hanging from the walls which are broken into niches, on each side of the frescos, containing the image of a Pope with angels and other allegorical figures. A list follows of the paintings with the artists responsible as suggested by Crowe and Cavalcaselle and largely confirmed by A. Venturi and others: To the left of the *Vision* is *St Peter Enthroned* between the *Church* and *Eternity* (perhaps executed by Giulio Romano assisted by Raffaellino del Colle); to the right is *Clement I* (by Giulio and Penni ?) between *Moderation* and *Comity*, of which the former is thought to be by Romano and Penni (see plate 158B); at the sides of the *Baptism* are *Damasus I*, between *Prudence* and *Peace* (all by Raffaellino), and *Leo I* (Penni) between *Purity* (Raffaellino) and *Truth* (Penni). Flanking the *Victory* is *Alexander I* (wrongly described in a scroll as Pope Sylvester and similar in style to *Clement I*), between *Faith* (Raffaellino ?) and *Religion* (Raffaellino ?); *Urban I* (Romano) is between *Justice* and *Charity* (Raffaellino or Romano). Next to the *Gift of Rome*: *Felix III* with the allegory of *Material Force* (both by Raffaellino) and *Gregory VII* with *Moral Force* (Raffaellino ?). On the pillars above are represented *Apollo and Diana* (Penni)—over the niche with *Damasus I*. The other male and female figures, bearing yokes and scrolls inscribed with the motto of Leo X, *SVAVE*, are mostly attributed to Raffaellino. In the imitation marble skirting a series of *caryatidae* bearing the emblems of the Medici family is interspersed, under the niches, with monochrome compartments simulating bronze and representing episodes from the life of Constantine. Under the *Baptism*: the *Order to Burn the Edicts against Christians* and the *Building of St Peter's* (Pope Sylvester here has the features of Clement VII; according to Vasari, Bramante and Leno are also visible in this fresco). Beneath the *Vision*: *Constantine's Camp near Rome*, in the larger compartment, and the *Entry into Rome* in the two smaller ones. Under the *Victory*: *Preparations for the Battle*, *Constantine Interrogating Prisoners* and the *Body of Maxentius Rescued from the River* in the three main compartments and the *Moving of a Camp* and the *Ship with Warriors Carrying the Head of Maxentius* in the two smaller ones. Beneath the *Gift of Rome*: the *Finding of the Cross*, *Sylvester I Healing Constantine from Leprosy* and *Constantine's Vision of the Apostles Peter and Paul*, which are all doubtfully attributed to Polidoro da Caravaggio. The embrasures of the windows contain other allegories such as *Constantine Encouraging Agriculture and Road-building*, *Constantine Encouraging Science and Art*, and historical subjects such as *Converted Pagans Destroying their Idols*, *St Sylvester Chaining a Dragon*, the *Meeting of Constantine and Helen* and *St Gregory Composing a Homily*, all of which are attributed to Perin del Vaga.

It is probable that, impressed with

the results achieved by Sebastiano del Piombo in mural oil-painting, Raphael decided to use this technique in the Chamber. For, among the allegories flanking the figures of Popes, *Justice* (plate 158A), *Moderation* and *Comity* (plate 158B), are painted in oils. On July 3, 1520— Raphael having died in April— Sebastiano himself mentioned one of these figures (see comment on plate 158A) in a letter. He referred to the figure as though it had just been completed at a time when the adjacent walls had not even begun to be decorated. But Raphael, before dying, had already executed or ordered the execution, under his personal supervision, of several preparatory drawings on the strength of which his apprentices begged Leo X to let them proceed with the decorations (this information is confirmed by another letter of Sebastiano dated September 6, 1520). Perhaps because the above-mentioned allegories (of which he only mentions two) were unsatisfactory, or else to avail themselves of traditional methods which were much quicker, the apprentices "threw on the floor the whole surface covered with mixture so that it could be treated with oils" (Vasari), sparing the figures already painted in the most important frescos by the major artists. The false vaulting, which replaced the original ceiling with rafters, was decorated in 1585, to the disadvantage of the mural paintings which had been intended for a totally different surrounding.

Plate 157

THE BATTLE OF CONSTANTINE. The largest part of this fresco is dedicated to the victorious charge of Constantine's army against the forces of Maxentius, which took place in A.D. 312 at Ponte Milvio, near Rome. The victor, whose figure seems inspired by Trajan in Rome's Arch of Constantine, is shown advancing towards his opponent. The latter, clinging to his horse in the Tiber, reminded Crowe and Cavalcaselle of the statues of the two *Dioscuri* in the Piazza del Quirinale, Rome. In the upper section, next to the window, Gamba noted the Villa Madama, which was then being built along lines devised by Raphael. In this case Raphael apparently directed the execution of Giulio Romano's cartoon and Romano was also responsible for its execution. The fresco is cracked and has been restored.

Plate 158A

JUSTICE. Crowe and Cavalcaselle drew attention to the fact that this fresco, flanking the image of Urban I, reveals a qualitative standard such as to confirm that Raphael, having provided the preliminary sketch and supervised the execution by Giulio Romano and Penni, did add a few touches of his own to the fresco. Modern critics, however, do not agree, because they see a contrast between this theory and Sebastiano del Piombo's letter of July 3, 1520, in which there is a possible reference to this figure, described by Raphael as the work of "the apprentices." One observes a noticeable darkening of colors, due to the oil technique.

Plate 158B

COMITY. This allegory, together with *Moderation*, appears on one side of the portrait of *Clement I*. Crowe and Cavalcaselle think that Raphael's work is even more evident in this fresco than in its twin illustration, *Moderation*, although they ascribe it to Pippi and Penni. Modern critics,

Gamba included, attribute the whole work to Giulio Romano. Here not only darkening, but indeed the very disappearance of color, mars the fresco's beauty, especially in the lower part.

Plate 158C

VISION OF THE CROSS. Before the battle against Maxentius, Constantine addresses his troops. In the skies above is a cross inscribed: "In this sign thou shalt conquer." In the opinion of Taja (*Descrizione del . . . Vaticano*, Rome, 1750), the dwarf in the foreground was included in the fresco to please Cardinal Ippolito de' Medici who was thus hoping to bestow immortality on his jester, Gradasso Berettai. In the background we see the Tiber, the Elio Bridge, and the mausoleums of Augustus and Hadrian. Both Vasari and Scannelli attribute this work to Pippi from sketches by Raphael—in which the dwarf and the two pages on the left do not appear. (There is, however, a *replica* on wood by Giulio Romano of the dwarf, in Le Puy Museum).

Plate 159A

GIFT OF ROME TO THE PAPACY. This fresco illustrates the legendary offer by Constantine to Pope Sylvester (here with the features of Clement VII) of temporal sovereignty, symbolized by a golden statuette of *Dea Roma*. Vasari noted the portraits of Giulio Romano— whom Crowe and Cavalcaselle identify as the man by the second column

to the right, about to remove his cap —of Castiglione, Pontano, Marullo and others. Bellori recognizes also a member of the Flavi family who was a Grand Master of the Order of St Gregory. Passavant attributes this work to Pippi. His opinion is accepted by subsequent critics, especially in so far as the foreground figures are concerned. Crowe and Cavalcaselle may be right in noting Raffaellino del Colle's style in the rest of the fresco. Extensive repaintings are noticeable.

Plate 159B

BAPTISM OF CONSTANTINE. The scene is set in the Lateran Basilica and Pope Sylvester has the features of a beardless Clement VII. The book held by the priest is inscribed: *Hodie salus Urbi et Imperio facta est.* Heading Constantine's attendants is his own son, Crispus. On the left, turning his back to the observer, is the man indicated by Vasari as Clement's favorite, Cavalierino. No preparatory drawings by Raphael seem to exist, but the conception is probably his. The smooth and colorless composition is almost universally ascribed to Penni, assisted perhaps by Pippi in the figures of Crispus and Cavalierino (Crowe and Cavalcaselle).

Plate 160

ENGRAVING BY RAIMONDI OF DECORATIONS IN THE HALL OF THE PALAFRENIERI. *Vatican.* See Lost Frescos.

LOST FRESCOS

CORRIDOR in the Vatican, 1511–14? Vasari notes that Baldassarre Peruzzi was entrusted by Julius II with decorating an aviary in "a corridor of the [Vatican] Palace," built a short time before "near the roof."

Here Baldassarre painted "all the months in chiaroscuro and the exercises which should be carried out in each month of the year." A document published by Muntz states that Julius II asked Raphael (June, 1511) to complete the decoration of this corridor before starting his work in the *Stanza d' Eliodoro*. It seems that during the reign of Julius Raphael painted one of the seventeen arches in the corridor, receiving for this work 200 ducats; under Leo X he painted four others, for which he was paid 400 ducats. Geymüller, quoted by Müntz, assumes that these frescos were intended for one of the two floors on the right side of the Belvedere courtyard. A great part of this building fell into ruin under Clement VII (Vasari), and probably Raphael's paintings perished with it. Steinmann's attempt to identify the aviary as the Vatican *Loggetta* above the *Logge* was proved mistaken.

ELEPHANT, 1516. King Manuel of Portugal sent Pope Leo X a gift of an elephant called Hanno which was greatly loved by the Pope. When it died, Raphael was ordered to portray it on one of the Vatican gates. The portrait was enriched by a solemn epitaph in Latin, later transcribed by Cancellieri (*Storia de' sommi pontefici*, Rome, 1802), and also recorded in a copy of the fresco by Francisco de Hollanda, in a notebook which is now visible in the Escurial, executed after 1538. In the inscription commemorating Raphael the date appears: MDXVI. 8 JVNII. From the copy, Crowe and Cavalcaselle argue that the painting was executed by Giulio Romano.

DECORATIONS, in the Hall of the *Palafrenieri*, Vatican, executed during the month of July, 1517? Vasari notes that Raphael "decorated one chamber in which there were some figures of apostles in earthenware and other saints inside tabernacles, and . . . Giovanni da Udine . . . reproduced all the animals owned by Pope Leo there." Vasari also records that the *Apostles* were executed "in chiaroscuro, as large as life and very beautiful." After the frescos had been mostly destroyed following the Hall's alterations decreed by Pius IV, these frescos were repainted from memory in 1560, by Taddeo and Federico Zuccari. The originals were engraved by Marcantonio Raimondi (*Bartsch*, vol. XIV, Nos. 64–76). Plate 160 reproduces a print from *St John the Evangelist*. Possibly a bill of payment of 20 ducats made out on July 1, 1517 (Rome, State Archives) to "Raphael's apprentices" is related to this work. The decorations were praised by Armenini (*De' veri precetti della pittura*, Rome, 1587). In the above-mentioned engravings certain features are discernible similar to the period of Raphael's cartoons for the Vatican tapestries. (See plate 160.)

FIRST LOGGIA in the Vatican, 1519. In a letter of March 4, 1519, from Rome, Michiel observes that Raphael "has decorated in the [Vatican] Palace . . . a very long *Loggia*, and is now decorating two more, which will be lovely things." The work done in the *loggia longhissima* must surely be Raphael's *Bible*. As far as the other two are concerned, it was assumed that the first one was the *Loggetta* on the third floor, and the second *Loggia*, on the ground floor, repainted by Alessandro Mantovani in the second half of 1800. Michiel wrote in his diary, on December 27, 1519: "At the present time the lowest of the three *Loggie* built in the Palace—they all face North-East towards Rome—has been finished. It is decorated with foliage, grotesques and other similar fantasies, all very vulgar and cheap, and certainly ostentatious. But in the one immediately above it, there are paintings of great grace and value, the drawings for which are by Raphael." Michiel's letter gives rise to some doubt: did his comparison between this *Loggia* and Raphael's *Bible* above it mean that the artist, having been entrusted with the work, had not even bothered to provide drawings for it? Or else, in his letter of March 4, was Michiel not referring to the lower *Loggia*? Or again, could it be that in the period between the two letters, the artists employed in the ground-floor were changed?

FRESCOS ATTRIBUTED TO RAPHAEL

FORTITUDE, other figures and lunette, 1500–4. We know that in 1500 Perugino began decorating the famous Hall of the Exchange in Perugia. A. Venturi (*Storia . . .*, VII, 2, Milan, 1913) thought that Raphael contributed to this enterprise and he assigned to the artist the allegory of *Fortitude* on the left wall and, on the right wall, the whole fresco of the *Eternal Father Between Two Angels and Cherubs* above a group of *Sibyls*. Venturi dated the first work 1500 and the second, 1504. This theory met with some success. Pittaluga (1955) seems to accept it at least in so far as *Fortitude* is concerned and Fischel attributes to Raphael *Fortitude* and the head of Solomon in the twin fresco. Venturi's attributions were recently again submitted (*Raffaello*, 1952) along with the arguments they had caused among critics. Previously Gamba, though admitting that Raphael, who was seventeen at the time, could well have contributed to the Exchange, observed: "It is improbable, however, that Perugino, committed to such an important work, would entrust a mere boy with figures, especially heads, of such eminence. In any case, there is no part of this work in which the Master's hand (Perugino) is not discernible, except for the ornaments on the ceiling." Modern critics (Ragghianti, Ortolani, Carli), while not rejecting the possibility that Raphael contributed to the cycle, are unable to single out any particular instance of his intervention.

STORIES OF ENEA PICCOLOMINI, 1502–06. On the strength of some vague references by Vasari, the theory is that Raphael contributed to the mural cycle of the Piccolomini Library at Siena, decorated by Pinturicchio between 1502 and 1506. This hypothesis is not confirmed by documents or stylistic evidence, and modern critics reject it almost unanimously with the possible exception of Fischel. Raphael may, however, have provided two cartoons for the Library: the *Meeting of Frederick III and Eleanor of Portugal*, now in the Bedeschi collection in Perugia and the *Departure of Piccolomini for the Council of Basel*, now in the Uffizi Gallery. Both cartoons are unreservedly assigned to Raphael by Fischel and Gamba.

LAST SUPPER, 1505. Some early scholars attributed to Raphael the *Last Supper* in the refectory of St Onophrius, a former convent of Franciscan nuns in Florence. This theory is still accepted, among others, by Young (*The Medici*, London, 1956) with the following proviso: "It is not certain whether Raphael painted the whole fresco or only that part which is signed [and dated 1505] by him." Crowe and Cavalcaselle along with numerous modern critics, however, rejected the attribution and insisted upon Perugino's authorship.

CHAPEL, *circa* 1519. Gamba recalls that Raphael instructed his pupils to decorate the apse of the papal hunt-

ing villa at Magliana, near Rome, with a *Martyrdom of St Cecilia*. This is now lost but a print of it by Raimondi reveals a striking similarity of style to Raphael's tapestries. Gamba notes also that the chapel's ceiling was decorated with a magnificent fresco of the *Eternal Father between Two Angels*, now exhibited at the Louvre. Crowe and Cavalcaselle believe that this work was originally to be seen in a niche above the altar, opposite a large lunette with an *Annunciation*. Two other lunettes might have depicted the *Meeting of Mary and Elizabeth* and the *Martyrdom of St Cecilia*. Crowe and Cavalcaselle attributed these four frescos to Francia, but claim that they were painted at two different times; the second and the fourth, which are replicas of works by Perugino, were done in 1505; the other two are much later, and were probably based on drawings by Raphael. The two latter frescos were acquired in 1873 by the French Government as original Raphaels, but a few years later only the *Eternal Father* was still on show at the Louvre. The *Martyrdom of St Cecilia*, definitely ascribed to Raphael by Passavant, had been put into storage. A. Venturi (*Storia . . .*, VII, 2, Milan, 1913) believes the Magliana frescos to have been painted by a mediocre follower of Perugino. He furthermore assigns to Pastura, an imitator of Spagna, the *Muses*, which were also part of the chapel's decorations. This last work has been connected by some with Raphael's *Parnassus*.

LOCATION OF FRESCOS

PERUGIA

CHURCH OF SAN SEVERO
Trinity and Saints (plates 2 and 3).

ROME

ACADEMY OF SAN LUCA
Figure of Boy (plate 91).

CHURCH OF SANT'AGOSTINO
Isaiah (plate 90).

CHURCH OF SANTA MARIA
DELLA PACE
Sibyls and Angels (plates 92–99).

VILLA FARNESINA
The Triumph of Galatea (plates 60–64 and color plate IV, Part 1). *The Lodge of Psyche* (plates 108–127).

VATICAN PALACES
Stanza della Segnatura: *Vault* (plates 4–7); *Dispute of the Sacrament* (plates 8–23 and color plates I, II, Part 1); *School of Athens* (plates 24–39 and color plate III, Part 1; Cartoon—plates 40–41—in the Pinacoteca Ambrosiana at Milan); *Parnassus* (plates 42–48); *Augustus Rescuing Vergil's Aeneid from the Fire* (plate 49A); *Alexander the Great Depositing the Poems of Homer in the Tomb of Achilles* (plate 49B); *Cardinal and Theological Virtues*

(plates 50–57); *Tribonian Handing the Code to Justinian* (plate 58); *Gregory IX Approving the Decretals* (plate 59).
Stanza d'Eliodoro: *Vault* (plates 65–67); *Expulsion of Heliodorus* (plates 68–71); *The Mass of Bolsena* (plates 72–79 and color plates V, VI, Part 2); *Repulsion of Attila* (plates 80–83); the *Liberation of St Peter* (plates 84–89).
Stanza dell'Incendio: *Fire in the Borgo* (plates 100–104 and color plates VII, VIII, Part 2); *Battle of Ostia* (plate 105); *Coronation of Charlemagne* (plate 106A); *Oath of Leo III before Charlemagne* (plate 106B).
Cardinal Bibbiena's Bathing Room: Decorations (plate 107).
Logge: *Stories from the Old and New Testaments* (plates 128–153); *Loggetta*: Decorations (plates 154–156).
Sala di Costantino: *Victory over Maxentius* (plate 157); *Allegories* (plates 158A and B); *Vision of the Cross* (plate 158C); *Gift of Rome to the Papacy* (plate 159A); the *Baptism of Constantine* (plate 159B).

URBINO

CASA SANTI
Madonna and Child (plate 1).

SELECTED CRITICISM

Those who bowed to Michelangelo were mostly sculptors who considered only his design and the tremendous power of his figures, and it seemed to them that Raphael's gracious and gentle manner was too facile. For they did not know that facility is the chief principle of excellence in any art, and the most difficult to achieve.

LOCOVICO DOLCE
Dialogo della pittura, Venice, 1557.

At times, the artist is a pure historian, at times a pure poet, and again at times he is both. When he is a pure poet, . . . he should be allowed to paint whatever he likes . . . of which we have an example in the Chigi Logge which Raphael decorated.

GIOVANNI ANDREA GILIO
Due dialoghi, Camerino, 1564.

His genius, however formed to blaze and shine might, like fire in combustible matter, forever have lain dormant, if it had not caught a spark by its contact with Michelangelo: and though it never burst out with his extraordinary heat and vehemence, yet it must be acknowledged to be a more pure, regular, and chaste flame. Though our judgment must upon the whole decide in favor of Raphael, yet he never takes such a firm hold and entire possession of the mind as to make us desire nothing else, and to feel nothing wanting.

JOSHUA REYNOLDS
Discourses on Art, circa 1780.

Everything in him bears the mark of facility. It is as if he never stops to think for a moment before painting; even his pictorial technique does not appear controlled by any calculation. His hand obeyed almost instinctively an extraordinary richness of ideas, so great as to allow no choice. Among all the possible aspects of an object Raphael chose the first one . . . hence his marvelous sobriety, his constant measure; no extravagance, no baseness, no triviality. I am not referring to what some critics believe they have discovered in a nose painted this or that way, more or less along the lines of classical rules—for none made freer use than Raphael of all Nature's forms. He ennobled the character of everything, from mere decoration to the relationship between the ensemble and its details.

EUGÈNE DELACROIX
in *Revue de Paris*, XI, 1830.

Whenever an artist resolves to challenge and overcome the difficulties of art for his own glorification we believe that he has preferred his love for himself to the right end. Therefore while we admire in Raphael's last works that which is difficult, in this we prefer them to the others. But we are more deeply moved by the effective and modest simplicity of the *Dispute of the Sacrament* which, however, is not lacking in subtlety of artifice, though we confess that Raphael's artifices are never excessive.

ANTONIO BIANCHINI
Del purismo nelle arti, circa 1836.

This *School of Athens* with its three companion pictures, which include in their historical development Theology, Poetry, and Jurisprudence, is the poem of culture, as vast as Dante's Paradise with the addition of Limbo.   FRANCESCO DE SANCTIS
Storia della letteratura italiana, Napoli, 1870.

The forms in the "Disputa" are noble in intention, as they always are in Raphael's best work. But think away the spaciousness of their surroundings. What has become of the solemn dignity, the glory that radiated from them? It has gone like divinity from a god. And the other fresco, the *School of Athens*, would suffer still more from such treatment. We have a cartoon of this subject with the figures only, and we have Raphael's painting. How ordinary and second-rate are the mere figures; how transformed when seen against those sublime arches, almost the grandest ever conceived! And not only are the figures ennobled, but yourself. How like a demigod you feel here in this lighter, purer air!

But there is in our civilization another element which, though it is certainly much less important in our conscious intellectual life, and of much less interest to the pictorial imagination, is said, nevertheless, to be morally superior and poetically grander—all the Hebraic element, I mean, that has come to us from the Old and New Testaments. Sanzio here, also, performed a task by which we have benefited ever since, for, imperturbably Hellenic in spirit, he has given an Hellenic garb to the Hebraic universe. In pictures which he either executed or superintended, or at least inspired, Raphael has completely illustrated both the Old and the New Testaments. . . . And this imagery, in which Raphael has clothed the Hebrew world for us, is no more Hebraic than that of Virgil, singing the new order of things when the lion shall lie down with the lamb. Raphael has brought about the extraordinary result that when we read even the Hebrew classics, we read them with an accompaniment of Hellenic imagery. What a power he has been in modern culture. Hellenizing the only force that could have thwarted it!

BERNARD BERENSON
The Italian Painters of the Renaissance (1897), London, 1957.

The *Dispute* and the *School of Athens* mark a further step in his artistic evolution so far as the composition and harmony of his groups are concerned. . . . The public finds it difficult, now-a-days,to consider and appreciate these works from such a point of view, being accustomed, by now, to look elsewhere for a painting's values: in the facial expressions, in the spiritual relationship —as it were—between the various characters.

The public would like to know, in the first place, what these figures mean and will not be satisfied until they are told their names . . . only very few feel that the essential value of such pictures is not to be sought in their details but in the harmonic fusion of their groups, in the rhythm imparted to the whole scheme. These are decorative creations of the highest order,

though I do not use here the term "decorative" in its ordinary sense: what I mean, in fact, is pictures whose essential value is not to be found in an isolated head nor in a psychological connection but in the way in which images are placed into space and in the relationship thereby established between them. Raphael knew as no one else before him what may be pleasing to the human eye.   HEINRICH WÖLFFLIN
Classical Art (1898), Florence, 1941.

If the fresco's didactic center [*School of Athens*] is provided by the gestures of Plato and Aristotle, its artistic center is the background. That architecture is neither Greek nor Roman. It is the architecture of Raphael's friend, Bramante. In order to find his own reality Raphael looks for the forms of his own time. How ample is this space in which the Greek philosophers breathe! This spacial magnitude expresses Raphael's ecstatic feeling when confronted with the heroes of ancient civilization. It is this ecstasy which impresses upon the figures something more than physical beauty, something rich transforms a summary of Greek philosophy into a legend. The harmonic rhythm of the arches, as well as the succession of groups of figures, expresses a nobility, a seriousness and a serenity born out of Raphael's admiration for Greek culture.   LIONELLO VENTURI
La pittura, Rome, 1947.

The depth of thought animating them [the *Segnatura* frescos], the admirable accomplishment of form achieved in it by Raphael make of this *Stanza* not only the moral testament of the Renaissance but also one of the sanctuaries of the human spirit, a manifesto of those eternal classical values of Humanism without which the word, civilization, remained just empty.

DEOCLECIO REDIG DE CAMPOS
Itinerario pittorico dei musei vaticani, Rome, 1954.

93

BIBLIOGRAPHICAL NOTE

Listed below, with some of the major monographs quoted in *Paintings*, are several important works on Raphael's frescos.

G. VASARI. *Le Vite . . .*, Florence 1550 and 1568; Milan 1942–9. (Edited by C. L. Ragghianti.)

G. P. BELLORI. *Descrizione delle immagini dipinte da Raffaello nelle camere del palazzo . . . Vaticano*, Rome 1695.

B. URBANI. *Memorie de' risarcimenti fatti nelle Stanze . . . dal . . . Maratti*, in the appendix to *Vite* by Bellori, Rome 1942.

L. PUNGILEONI. *Elogio storico di Raffaello*, Urbino 1829.

I. D. PASSAVANT. *Raffael . . .*, Leipzig 1839 and 1858; Paris 1860; Florence 1882–91.

W. SCHERER. *Ueber Raphaels Schule von Athen*, Vienna 1872.

H. GRIMM. *Leben Raffaels*, Berlin 1872, 1913 and 1941.

J. A. CROWE and G. B. CAVALCASELLE. *Raphael*, London 1882–5; Florence 1884–91.

E. MÜNTZ. *Raphaël, sa vie, son œuvre et son temps*, Paris 1886 and 1900.

A. ROSENBERG and G. GRONAU. *Raffael*, Stuttgart and Leipzig 1909 and 1923.

U. GNOLI. *Gli affreschi del Cambio a Perugia*, in "Rassegna d'arte," 1913.

A. VENTURI. *Raffaello*, Urbino 1920; Milan–Verona (1935); Milan 1952 (with amendments by L. Venturi).

V. WAUSCHER. *Raphael*, London 1921.

A. VENTURI. *Storia dell'arte italiana*, IX, 2, Milan 1926.

N. TARCHIANI. *Raffaello. Le Logge*. Florence 1926.

M. T. TOZZI. *La volta della Stanza della Segnatura*, in "L'arte," 1927.

F. HERMANIN. *La Farnesina*, Bergamo 1927; Rome 1930.

G. GOMBOSI. *Sodoma und Peruzzi Urteil in der Deckenmalerei der Stanza della Segnatura*, in "Atti del II Congresso nazionale di studi romani," 1931.

C. GAMBA. *Raphaël*, Paris 1932.

M. FLUGI D'ASPERMONT. *Le Stanze di Raffaello*, supplement to "Illustrazione vaticana," 1934.

O. FISCHEL. "Santi, Raffaello," in *Allgemeines Lexikon* by Thieme and Becker, Leipzig 1935 (with extensive bibliography).

P. D'ANCONA. *La Stanza della Segnatura*, Bergamo 1937.

S. ORTOLANI. *Raffaello*, Bergamo 1942, 1946 and 1948 (with bibliography).

M. L. GENGARO. *Raffaello. La Stanza della Segnatura*, Bergamo 1944.

G. HOOGEWERFF. *Raffaello nella villa Farnesina*, in "Capitolium," 1945.

D. REDIG DE CAMPOS. *Raffaello e Michelangelo*, Rome 1946.

O. FISCHEL. *Raphael*, London 1948.

D. REDIG DE CAMPOS. *Le Stanze di Raffaello*, Florence 1950.

D. REDIG DE CAMPOS. *Itinerario pittorico del musei vaticani*, Rome 1954.

P. D'ANCONA. *Gli affreschi della Farnesina*, Milan 1955.

H. W. HEGEMANN. *Disputa und Schule von Athen*, Munich 1956.

REPRODUCTIONS

ACKNOWLEDGEMENT FOR PLATES

Anderson, Rome: plates 2–14, 16–50, 52–55, 59–64, 66–95, 98, 100–6, 106B, 109–29, 157, 158, 159B. *Alinari, Florence:* 1, 15, 51, 56–58, 65, 96, 97, 99, 106A, 130–53, 159A. *Vasari, Rome:* 108. *Scala, Florence:* color plates I, II, III, IV (Part 1), VII, VIII (Part 2). *The remaining plates supplied by private sources.*

Plate 65. CEILING OF STANZA D'ELIODORO,
Rome, Vatican

Plate 66. *Details of plate 65*

Plate 67. *Details of plate 65*

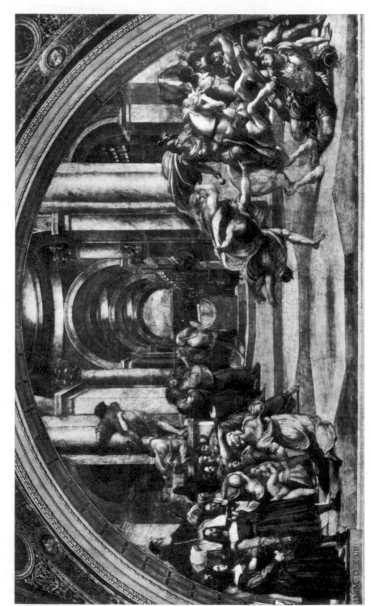

Plate 68. THE EXPULSION OF HELIODORUS, Rome, Vatican

Plate 69. *Detail of plate 68*

Plate 70. *Detail of plate 68*

Plate 71. *Detail of plate 68*

Plate 72. THE MASS OF BOLSENA, Rome, Vatican

Plate 73. *Detail of plate 72*

Plate 74. *Detail of plate 72*

Plate 75. *Detail of plate 72*

Plate 76. *Detail of plate 72*

Plate 77. *Detail of plate 72*

Plate 78. *Detail of plate 72*

Plate 79. *Detail of plate 72*

Plate 80. THE REPULSION OF ATTILA,
Rome, Vatican

THE MASS OF BOLSENA,
Rome, Vatican
(*detail of plate 72*)

Plate 81. *Detail of plate 80*

Plate 82. *Detail of plate 80*

Plate 83. *Detail of plate 80*

Plate 84. THE LIBERATION OF ST PETER,
Rome, Vatican

Plate 85. *Detail of plate 84*

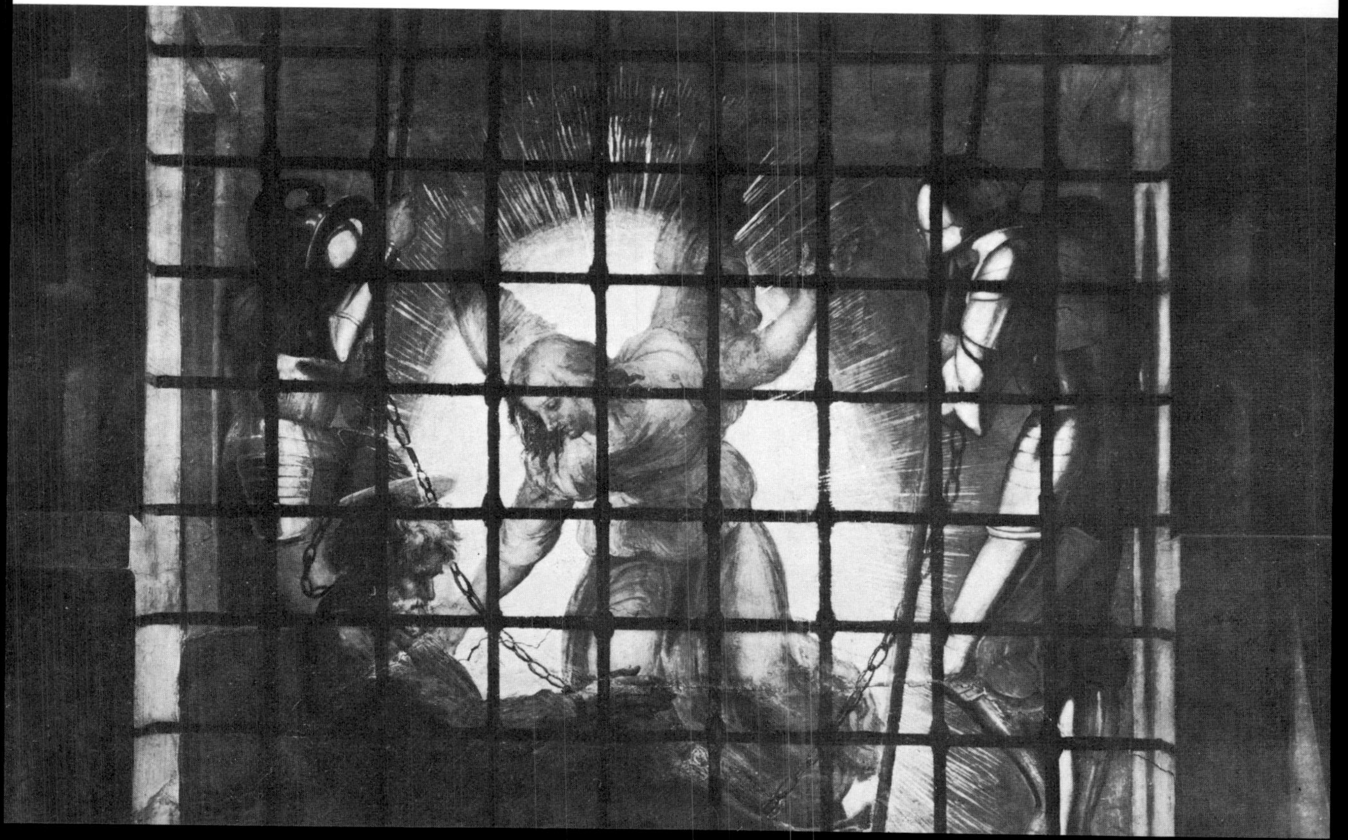

Plate 86. *Detail of plate 84*

Plate 87. *Detail of plate 84*

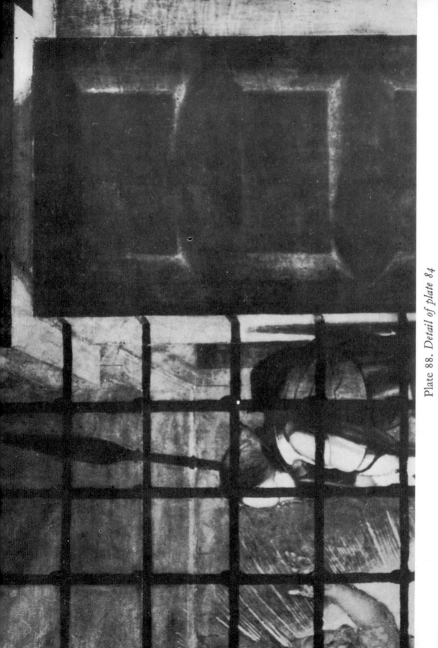

Plate 88. *Detail of plate 84*

Plate 89. *Detail of plate 84*

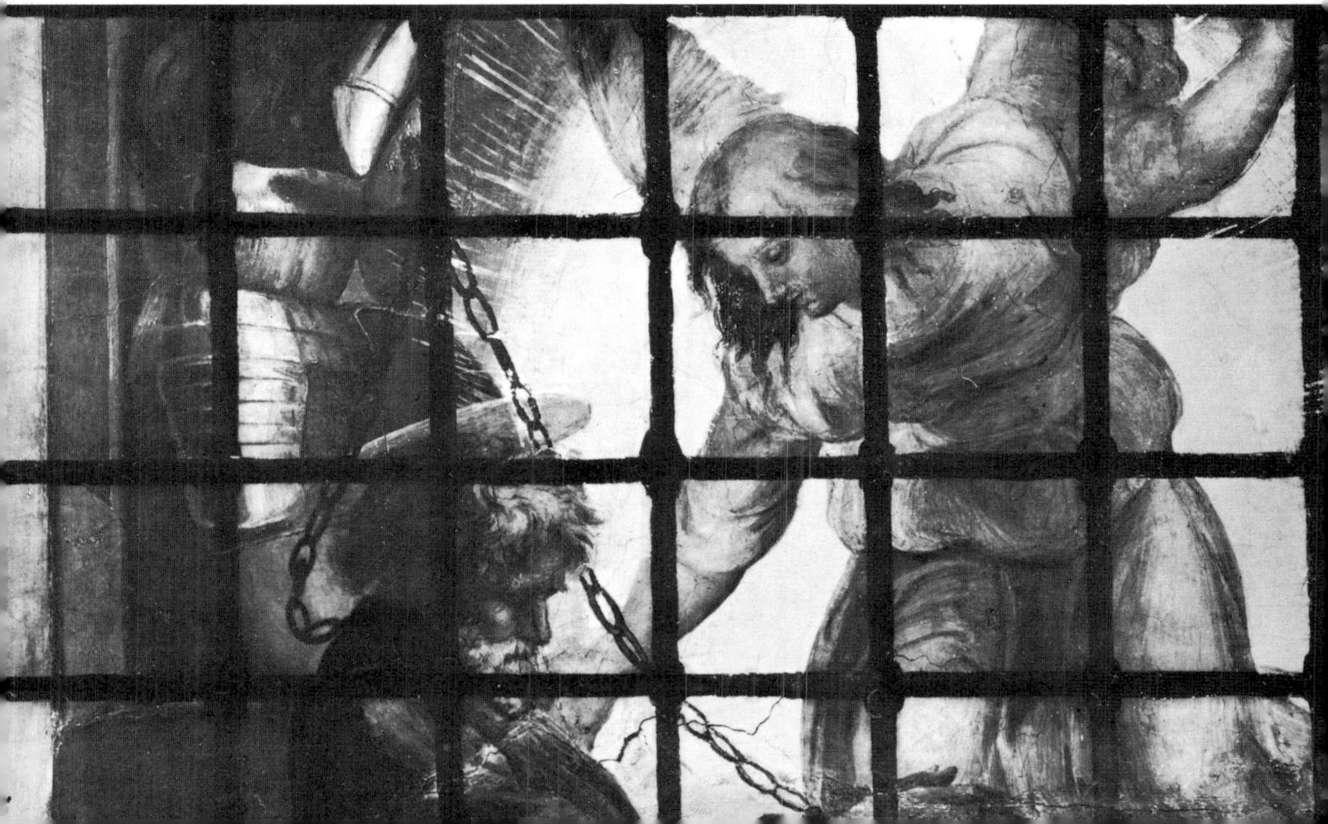

Plate 90. ISAIAH,
Rome, Church of Sant'Agostino

Plate 91. CHERUB,
Rome, San Luca Academy

Plate 92. SYBILS AND ANGELS,
Rome, Church of Santa Maria della Pace

Plate 93. *Detail of plate 92*

Plate 94. *Detail of plate 92*

Plate 95. *Detail of plate 92*

Plate 96. *Detail of plate 92*

THE MASS OF BOLSENA,
Rome, Vatican
(*detail of plate 72*)

Plate 97. *Detail of plate 92*

Plate 98. *Detail of plate 92*

Plate 99. *Detail of plate 92*

Plate 100. FIRE IN THE BORGO, Rome, Vatican

Plate 101. *Detail of plate 100*

Plate 102. *Detail of plate 100*

Plate 103. *Detail of plate 100*

Plate 104. *Detail of plate 100*

Plate 105. THE BATTLE OF OSTIA,
Rome, Vatican

Plate 106. THE CORONATION OF CHARLEMAGNE *and*
THE OATH OF LEO III, Rome, Vatican

Plate 107. DECORATIONS IN CARDINAL BIBBIENA'S BATHROOM,
Rome, Vatican

Plate 108. THE LODGE OF PSYCHE,
Rome, Villa Farnesina

Plate 109. VENUS AND CUPID, Rome, Villa Farnesina

Plate 110. CUPID AND THE GRACES, Rome, Villa Farnesina

Plate III. VENUS WITH CERES AND JUNO, Rome, Villa Farnesina

Plate 112. VENUS IN A GOLD CHARIOT, Rome, Villa Farnesina

FIRE IN THE BORGO,
Rome, Vatican
(*detail of plate 100*)

Plate 113. VENUS AND JOVE, Rome, Villa Farnesina

Plate 114. MERCURY, Rome, Villa Farnesina

Plate 115. PSYCHE RETURNING FROM THE STYX, Rome, Villa Farnesina

Plate 116. VENUS AND PSYCHE,
Rome, Villa Farnesina

Plate 117. CUPID AND JOVE,
Rome, Villa Farnesina

Plate 118. MERCURY AND PSYCHE, Rome, Villa Farnesina

Plate 119. WINGED BOY AND EAGLE AND
WINGED BOY WITH TRIDENT, Rome, Villa Farnesina

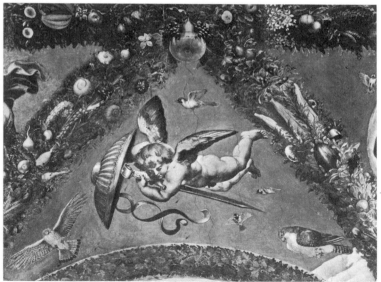

Plate 120. WINGED BOYS WITH CERBERUS AND
WINGED BOY WITH ARMS, Rome, Villa Farnesina

Plate 121. WINGED BOY WITH GRIFFIN AND
WINGED BOY WITH CADUCEUS, Rome, Villa Farnesina

Plate 122. WINGED BOY WITH PANTHER AND
WINGED BOY WITH REED PIPE, Rome, Villa Farnesina

Plate 123. WINGED BOYS WITH SHIELD AND HELMET, Rôme, Villa Farnesina

Plate 124. WINGED BOYS WITH HARPY AND
WINGED BOY WITH CROCODILE, Rome, Villa Farnesina

Plate 125. WINGED BOY, LION AND SEA-HORSE *and*
WINGED BOY WITH BOW, Rome, Villa Farnesina

Plate 126. THE COUNCIL OF THE GODS, Rome, Villa Farnesina

Plate 127. THE WEDDING BANQUET, Rome, Villa Farnesina

Plate 128. EPISODES FROM THE CREATION, Rome, Vatican

FIRE IN THE BORGO,
Rome, Vatican
(*detail of plate 100*)

Plate 129. EPISODES FROM THE CREATION, Rome, Vatican

Plate 130. THE STORY OF ADAM AND EVE, Rome, Vatican

Plate 131. THE STORY OF ADAM AND EVE, Rome, Vatican

Plate 132. NOAH AND THE ARK, Rome, Vatican

Plate 133. NOAH AND THE ARK, Rome, Vatican

Plate 134. THE STORY OF ABRAHAM, Rome, Vatican

Plate 135. ABRAHAM AND THE ANGELS *and*
THE FLIGHT OF LOT, Rome, Vatican

Plate 136. THE STORY OF ISAAC, Rome, Vatican

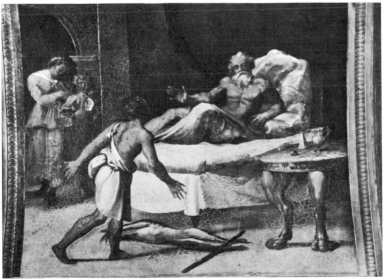

Plate 137. THE STORY OF ISAAC, Rome, Vatican

Plate 138. THE STORY OF JACOB, Rome, Vatican

Plate 139. THE STORY OF JACOB, Rome, Vatican

Plate 140. THE STORY OF JOSEPH, Rome, Vatican

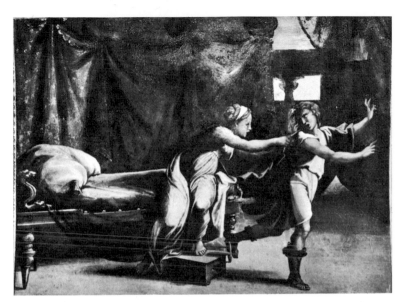

Plate 141. THE STORY OF JOSEPH, Rome, Vatican

Plate 142. THE STORY OF MOSES, Rome, Vatican

Plate 143. THE STORY OF MOSES, Rome, Vatican

Plate 144. THE STORY OF MOSES, Rome, Vatican

Plate 145. THE STORY OF MOSES, Rome, Vatican

Plate 146. THE STORY OF JOSHUA, Rome, Vatican

Plate 147. THE STORY OF JOSHUA, Rome, Vatican

Plate 148. THE STORY OF DAVID, Rome, Vatican

Plate 149. THE STORY OF DAVID. Rome, Vatican

Plate 150. THE STORY OF SOLOMON, Rome, Vatican

Plate 151. THE STORY OF SOLOMON, Rome, Vatican

Plate 152. THE STORY OF JESUS, Rome, Vatican

Plate 153. THE STORY OF JESUS, Rome, Vatican

Plate 154. THE VATICAN LOGGETTA

Plate 155. DECORATIONS IN THE VATICAN LOGGETTA

Plate 156. DECORATIONS IN THE VATICAN LOGGETTA

Plate 157. THE BATTLE OF CONSTANTINE,
Rome, Vatican

Plate 158. JUSTICE, COMITY *and* THE VISION OF THE CROSS,
Rome, Vatican

Plate 159. THE GIFT OF ROME *and* THE BAPTISM OF CONSTANTINE, Rome, Vatican

Plate 160. ENGRAVING BY RAIMONDI OF DECORATIONS
IN THE VATICAN HALL OF THE PALAFRENIERI